DATE DUE

JA 7 '94			
NO 20 '94			
DE 2 94			
FE 08			
MY 24 '83			

DEMCO 38-296

DROUGHT

EDWARD F. DOLAN

DROUGHT

THE PAST, PRESENT, AND FUTURE ENEMY

Franklin Watts ○ *1990*
New York ○ *London* ○ *Toronto* ○ *Sydney*

Illustrations and map by: Vantage Art

Photographs courtesy of: Photo Researchers: pp. 2, 13 (Jim Balog) 35
(David Frazier), 53 (John Bova), 69 (Bordes/Explorer), 82
(Science Source), 90 (Jeff Lepore), 95
(Bill Belknap), 125 (Porterfeil/Chickering), 129 (Lawrence Migdale);
Food and Agricultural Organization: p. 18;
USDA/Soil Conservation Service: pp. 31, 80, 91.

Library of Congress Cataloging-in-Publication Data

Dolan, Edward F., 1924–
Drought : the past, present, and future enemy / by Edward F. Dolan :
[illustrations and map by Vantage Art].
p.   cm.
Includes bibliographical references.
Summary: Discusses the causes and effects of droughts and examines
the possibility of future droughts due to such phenomena as the
greenhouse effect. Also discusses weather modification as a
solution to this problem.
ISBN 0-531-10900-3
1. Droughts. [1. Droughts.] I. Title.
QC929.D8D65   1990
551.57'73—dc20   89-25016 CIP   AC

CONTENTS

---○---

DROUGHT

CHAPTER ONE

○

DROUGHT: PORTRAIT OF THE ENEMY

The year is 1936. You and your parents are standing on the front porch of your Kansas farmhouse. The land that your family has long farmed here on the American Great Plains stretches away into the far distance. It once shimmered with the golden glow of wheat at this time of year. But now it lies barren, with not a planting to be seen. The ground is hard and cracked. There has been little or no rain here since 1932—and little or no rain throughout all of the Great Plains, which make their way eastward from the Rocky Mountains to the Mississippi River and just beyond, and south from the Canadian border to Texas. Your parents can no longer make a living on this land. They'll soon be taking you to some other part of the country where your father may be able to find work. As you travel, you'll see that thousands of other farm families are on the road with you, all uprooted by what the rainless years have done.

The year is 1973. You live in the Sahel, the vast region that stretches across northern Africa just below the Sahara Desert and takes in eight countries, from

Senegal on the west to Sudan on the east. The other countries within the Sahelian zone are, from west to east, Mauritania, Mali, Upper Volta, Niger, Nigeria, and Chad. The climate is hot and dry. It rains here only when the monsoon rains arrive each summer. But for five years now they have stayed away. The land is parched. Crops cannot grow. The wells have run dry. Countless people and animals have died. You yourself are weak from hunger and thirst. You, too, will die in a few days.

The year is 1988. Your home is in the San Francisco Bay area of northern California. Unlike the Sahel, this is an area rich in rain. But you're in the second year in which the rainfall has been far below normal. There is the danger that your reservoirs and rivers will soon run dry. People are talking of programs to conserve water—programs that will allow each family to use only so much water, programs that will see lawns go unwatered and baths not taken daily.

In each of these instances, you are caught in the grip of the weather phenomenon called *drought*.[1] Also known in some areas as *drowt* or *drough* (but pronounced *drowt*), it is an enemy feared throughout the world. It attacks and depletes our supply of the element that, along with the air we breathe, is necessary for the survival of all plant and animal life on our planet: water.

The term drought comes from the old Anglo-Saxon word *drugath*, which means "dry." In the years since the Anglo-Saxons (a Germanic people) dominated England in the Middle Ages the word has been expanded to denote dry weather. The word, however, can be defined in several ways. Two of the most often-heard definitions are:

- The condition that arises when the average rainfall for an area drops far below the normal amount for an extended period of time

- The condition that results from a prolonged period of dry weather in which the water needs of plants and animals are not met

Both definitions are simple ones. So is the one used by the National Weather Service of the United States: a period of twenty-one days or more when the rainfall is only 30 percent of the average rainfall for a particular locale and season. The simplest of all, however, is to be found in most dictionaries. Using just three words, they describe drought as "prolonged dry weather."

The words *extended* and *prolonged* are vital to the definitions. They separate droughts from those rainless periods called "dry spells." Many people believe dry spells and droughts are the same, but the two are quite distinct from each other. Dry spells do not do as much damage as droughts. They are usually defined as periods of four to about fourteen days when there is no measurable amount of rain. Dry spells begin to be classified as droughts when they last three weeks or more.

Simple though these definitions may be, drought itself is anything but a simple phenomenon. It has many faces.

An Insidious Enemy

Drought is an insidious enemy.[2] It sneaks up on us. Unlike such other weather dangers as hurricanes, tornadoes, and electrical storms, it does not strike in a sudden, roaring fury and last for just minutes or hours. Rather, it comes quietly in the cheerful guise of clear, sunny skies and then remains to work its damage just as quietly over a period of weeks, months, or even years. Its stealth can delude us into making tragic errors.

At first, because we are enjoying the fine weather, we often do not realize that drought is in our midst until it inflicts so much damage that it can no longer be ignored. Once we do recognize its presence, we often make the mistake of thinking it cannot possibly hang about much longer. Rain will surely put an end to it soon. Nursing this hope, we often contribute to the harm being done. We delay too long in enacting measures that will help us conserve our dwindling supply of water.

All the while, rivers, streams, and wells—no longer replenished by rain and melting snow—begin to run dry. Likewise, the water that nature keeps stored in the ground is lost through evaporation. The soil turns dry and hard under a coating of dust. Plants wither and die. Animals begin to die of thirst and—since there is no longer enough plant life on which to feed—starvation. Given sufficient time to run completely out of water, we, too, face death.*

As matters worsen, other dangers appear. The weather produces dry conditions that make forest and grass fires a daily threat. The dryness can gen-

---

* Humans need to consume about 2½ quarts (2.3 l) of water per day. We take in about 1½ quarts (1.4 l) from the liquids we drink, with the remaining quart being provided by the water content in our foods. Our bodies are made up of about 95 to 98 percent water. This works out to about 30 quarts (28 l) or 114 pounds (51.3 kg) if you're a young person weighing 120 pounds (54 kg). Lose as little as 12 percent of that body water and your life is endangered.

A river's water level hits a dramatic low during a recent drought that hit southwestern Idaho.

erate hard winds that will send the parched soil whipping into the air in blinding dust storms. These storms—nicknamed "black blizzards" and "dusters"—are a particular menace in farm areas where the topsoil has been loosened by years of plowing. Some of the worst occurred during the drought that plagued the American Great Plains in the 1930s. These storms carried dust thousands of feet into the air and turned night into day for hours at a time. One such blizzard sent clouds of dust billowing eastward beyond New York City and out over the Atlantic Ocean.

A Complex Enemy

Drought is one of the most complex forces in nature, and its causes are many. Moreover, drought is divided into several types. Further, it can strike a region, a country, a cluster of countries, an entire continent, or several continents. It can attack any time of the year and remain on the scene for any length of time. When it strikes, it can raise havoc in one area and completely spare another area a short distance away.

An Enemy of Many Faces ○ Finally, drought is a force that means different things to different people. For example, suppose that you live in an area where the rainfall averages 23 inches (57.5 cm) per year; if one year brings only 10 inches (25 cm), you will know full well that your area has been caught in a drought. But suppose your homeland averages just 5 inches (12.5 cm) inches of rain annually. For you, when one year brings 10 inches, the rain will be more than abundant.

Using the same examples, suppose that several years bring 21 inches (52.5 cm) of rain to the region that annually averages 23 inches. The lost 2 inches (5 cm) may hardly be felt at all. But lose 2 inches of rain for two or three consecutive years in the area where the annual average is 5 inches and you will be facing disaster.

Because of these factors, the definitions we've given for drought are vaguely worded (except the one used by the National Weather Service). They speak only of a *prolonged* or *extended* period of *dry weather*. They do not specify exactly *how* prolonged or extended the period, or *how* dry the weather. They cannot do so because drought means so many different things to so many different people. What is called a drought in one place will not be considered a drought in another place.

Drought's Varying Touch ○ The complex nature of drought can perhaps best be seen in the diversity of ways that drought affects us. At the very least, it can present us with mere inconvenience; we're called on to conserve our remaining water by not taking daily showers and not flushing toilets after every use. This was the case in late 1988 when the people of northern California were living through their second year of below-average rains.

At the opposite end of the scale, it can do much harm as crops and livestock die for want of nourishment. The results can be disastrous for everyone. The disaster begins with the farmers and ranchers. Without crops to sell, the farmers must dig into their savings to buy seed for future plantings. Livestock must be sold off at reduced prices because the animals are scrawny with hunger. Finally, many families must leave their homes and seek work elsewhere—some because they no longer have any money to make the mortgage payments on their property, some because they are beginning to starve and know they no longer can survive where they are. This was the fate that befell thousands of American farmers and ranchers during the great drought of the 1930s.

From the farms and ranches, the hardship fans out to touch people in all walks of life. To see what happens, let's turn again to the northern California drought of 1988. It was part of a greater drought that extended throughout California and spread eastward across the country that year.[3] This nationwide drought struck especially hard at farm production in the midwestern and northeastern sections of the nation. The corn crop plunged by 43 percent; the barley crop went down 42 percent; oats, 43 percent; and spring wheat, a catastrophic 51 percent.

The U.S. government estimated that these reductions amounted to a loss of about $5 billion to $15 billion. Consequently, consumers were forced to pay more at the local market for food staples; this occurred because prices always rise when needed goods are scarce. Further, every taxpayer was handed an additional financial burden when Congress had to enact a $3.9 billion bill to help the stricken areas.

Such consequences are not limited to the country in which a drought occurs. In the early 1970s, the vast farmlands of the Soviet Union were hit by severe droughts that cost the nation millions of tons of wheat and other grains.[4] The USSR had to turn to the United States, Canada, and Australia for help, purchasing from them more than 13.55 million tons (12.3 million metric tons) of grains between 1972 and

1975. In 1972 alone, the United States agreed to sell the Soviet Union some $750 million worth of various grains over a three-year period. These purchases put a heavy strain on the Soviet treasury and, though they served as a financial boon for the U.S., Canada, and Australia, they greatly reduced the grain that the three countries keep stored for emergency use. For example, the 1972 purchase of U.S. grains involved one-fourth of the American wheat supply.

Drought also hurts all other industries that use water to manufacture their products. They must either curtail production to save water or develop expensive facilities that will enable them to operate with less water. Either action could result in job cutbacks and higher prices for commodities.

A Deadly Enemy

Worst of all, drought can cause death. Over the centuries, countless people have felt its fatal touch. Some, especially the very young and the very old, have been unable to withstand the terrible heat it brings. Some have died from the stress of seeing their life's work reduced to ruin. Death, however, takes its greatest toll when drought leads to famine. The loss of water, crops, and livestock becomes so great that starvation can stalk a region, a country, or a continent. The lives of hundreds of thousands or even millions of people are at risk.

The Sahel drought of the late 1960s and 1970s provides a terrible example of what a drought-induced famine can do.[5] By 1973, more than 100,000 Sahelian people and several million cattle (more than one third of the region's cattle) had died. Until food began pouring in from the outside world at year's

A man draws water for his cattle in Senegal, a region where drought-induced winds have caused sand dunes to move inland and threaten cultivated areas.

end, the United Nations estimated that as many as 6 million people might eventually have died.

The Sahel was not the only African region to suffer drought in the 1970s. Drought attacked throughout the continent during that decade and into the 1980s. By 1984, more than 150 million people in twenty-four African nations were facing starvation. Families everywhere abandoned their homes to seek food. By early 1985, an estimated 10 million Africans were on the road in search of food.

Deadly Comparisons ○ Its ability to kill in great numbers makes drought one of the deadliest—if not *the* deadliest—of all natural hazards. As if the examples of what it did in Sahel and the rest of Africa are not enough to prove the point, let's compare the number of lives lost to drought with those struck down by nature's other terrifying elements.[6]

Take, for a start, lightning storms and hurricanes. Lightning is said to flash about 8 million times a day in the world. Yet those 8 million flashes kill only about 200 people each year. One of the worst hurricanes in U.S. history struck Galveston, Texas, in 1900, killing 6,000 people. The U.S. drought of 1988 and the intense heat that accompanied it claimed 5,000 to 10,000 lives.

Or consider earthquakes and floods. Two of the most devastating quakes in recorded history both occurred in China—in 1556 and 1976; they took 830,000 and 800,000 lives respectively. In 1931, China suffered one of the world's greatest killer floods; left dead in its wake were an estimated 3.7 million people. But when drought took hold of China in 1877 and 1878, the resulting famine claimed approximately 9.5 million lives.

A Constant Enemy

Drought has been with us for millions of years—ever since our planet's atmosphere formed. It strikes somewhere on earth every year, and is present virtually every single day in the world's hot and dry deserts. Even in the best of times, drought causes American farmers to lose between 100 million and 500 million bushels of grain annually.[7]

Though drought has always plagued the world, it struck particularly hard in the 1970s and 1980s, as can be seen by looking no farther than Africa and the United States. The droughts experienced by these two areas have been matched at the same time in such widely separated countries as Canada, Italy, China, and New Zealand. Between 1961 and 1975, the Soviet Union suffered a drought almost every other year. Even England, which is famous for its rainy weather, went through a severe drought in 1976;[8] in June of that year, the British newspapers were calling it the worst stretch of dryness in 100 years; by September, it was elevated to the worst in 500 years.

These droughts have severely damaged the global food supply, including Italy's grape crop and New Zealand's sheep production. Hardest hit of all have been the vital crops of wheat, corn, and other grains.[9] In late 1988, the U.S. Department of Agriculture estimated that, unless the weather improved, the world's grain supply would last a mere sixty-two days by the time of the 1989 harvests.

Current predictions hold that the situation will worsen if drought goes on plaguing the world during the 1990s, especially if grain harvests in the United States continue to plunge as they did in 1988.

The United States, along with such countries as Canada and China, is one of the chief providers of grain for the world. Should the harvests of the major grain producers prove meager in the 1990s, and should the global population continue to grow at its present rate, we will face food shortages not only in the countries that have already suffered famine but everywhere in the world. All of us will feel their grim presence.

A Frightening Future ○ The future looms as even more alarming when we hear what weather and environmental experts are saying today. They believe the situation will indeed worsen. They predict that the world is standing on the threshhold of a period of extensive and persistent droughts.

The experts point to certain climatic and man-made factors that may well cause drought to play a greater and more dreadful role in our lives in future years. One such factor is the "greenhouse effect," which is thought to be gradually raising atmospheric temperatures throughout the world. Another factor is our always heavy and often indiscriminate use of water.

Because it threatens to affect our lives so greatly, drought is a subject that needs the attention of everyone. We must be fully aware of what it can do to us and our planet. Only then will we be able to take the steps necessary to protect ourselves and all the life around us from its awful touch.

To help prepare for the future, this book examines four areas:

○ The nature of drought: the basic facts about the way it works and the types into which it can be divided

- The history of drought and the history of the safeguards that humans have developed to help protect themselves against it
- The factors that may soon make drought play an even more frightening role in our lives than ever before
- The steps that we—as nations, groups, and individuals—must take to protect ourselves against the dangers threatened by an increasing number of droughts in the future

We turn now to the first topic—the nature of this age-old and ever-present enemy.

CHAPTER TWO

———○———

THE NATURE
OF THE ENEMY

To learn the nature of drought, we need to answer two questions: How exactly does drought come about? Does drought come in different forms?

How Drought Works

Drought works its damage by disrupting the smooth operation of what is called the hydrologic cycle.[1] This cycle, more commonly known as the water cycle, has been going on ever since our planet's atmosphere was formed some 4 billion years ago.* The

---

* The atmosphere, consisting of oxygen and other elements, extends out from the earth's surface for a distance of more than 500 miles (800 km), with its oxygen content dwindling as it ascends. Counting upward from the earth's surface, there are five layers: first, the troposphere, which contains the greatest concentration of oxygen and ranges up to distances of six to twelve miles; next, the stratosphere, extending another thirty miles or so; then the mesosphere and thermosphere, rising one after the other to the exosphere, which begins at an altitude of about 500 miles and reaches out into space. All the world's weather—including the conditions that generate droughts—occurs within the first atmospheric layer.

cycle continually sends water skyward as an invisible vapor, transforms it back into water far above our heads, and then returns it to earth.

Sent skyward is water vapor from the world's oceans, lakes, rivers, streams, wells, puddles, plants, and animals (including humans). Rising with it is vapor from the ground underfoot. On completing its upward journey, the vapor is then returned to earth in the form of precipitation. *Precipitation* is a general term that refers to moisture that falls from clouds. Meteorologists list rain, drizzle, snow, freezing rain, and hail as types of precipitation.

The Hydrologic Cycle ○ Each turn of the cycle begins with a process that has a tongue-twister of a name: *evapotranspiration*. The name combines two terms: *evaporation* and *transpiration*.

Evaporation is the process by which the warmth at the earth's surface (a warmth generated by the sun's heat that the earth has absorbed and is now sending back into the air) causes the water in everything from oceans to body perspiration to "disappear," that is, to turn into vapor for the skyward trip.

Transpiration is the process by which plants and animals give up their moisture content. Moisture seeps out from the surface mechanisms and internal organs of plants, and from membranes and pores in the bodies of animals. Once the moisture comes in contact with the air, evaporation takes over and transforms all or a portion of it into vapor.

Evapotranspiration distributes vast amounts of moisture into the air. Circulated into the atmosphere in every minute is about 3.1 billion cubic miles (12.7 billion cubic km) of water. About 84 percent of the rising moisture evaporates from the oceans; the re-

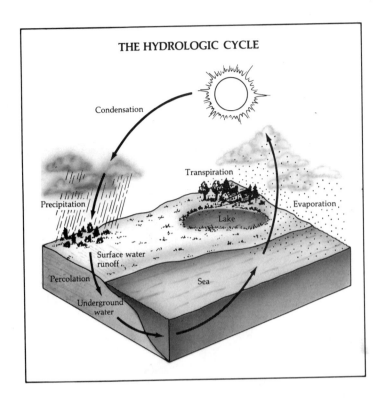

THE HYDROLOGIC CYCLE

Condensation

Transpiration

Precipitation

Evaporation

Lake

Surface water runoff

Percolation

Sea

Underground water

The hydrologic cycle is water in motion. Worldwide, millions of cubic miles of water are endlessly recycled from the ocean to the atmosphere to land, and back to the ocean again. All phases of the cycle are interrelated, such that altering the quantity of water in any phase—whether it is water in the form of rain, or water in a river, or groundwater beneath the surface— produces a change in other parts of the cycle. Human activities, such as land plowing, overgrazing, cutting of forests, and the building of reservoirs, have an impact on the exchange of moisture between land and atmosphere.

maining moisture comes from rivers, streams, plants, animals, and the ground. Of the 84 percent of rising moisture that evaporates from the oceans, only 75 percent of moisture that returns as precipitation falls into the oceans. The difference is made up by water flowing back into the oceans from rivers, glaciers, and the earth itself.

The rising water vapor eventually reaches the thin, cold air found at higher elevations. There it cools and, as a result, is condensed—turned back into water. The water shapes itself as tiny droplets that gather together in clouds or fog. (Fog is actually a low cloud, one so low that it touches the ground.) Then, because they are almost weightless, they float along on the wind. When the conditions aloft cause the droplets to become too heavy to be borne along on the wind, gravity takes over and they fall to earth as some form of precipitation, such as rain or snow. On gathering together in a cloud, water droplets range in size from 0.00008 to 0.001 inch (0.00002 to 0.0025 cm) in diameter. To fall as just one type of precipitation—rain—they must grow to diameters between 0.04 and 0.2 inches (0.1 and 0.5 cm).

A process called *coalescence* enables the droplets to gain enough weight to fall as precipitation. There are two types of coalescence. The first type occurs when the winds within a cloud—especially when a storm is brewing—become especially strong and whip the droplets about so furiously that they crash into each other. On colliding, they meld and remain together as larger droplets which in turn grow still larger by crashing into and melding with other droplets. At last, the droplets reach a weight great enough to overcome the winds that have hitherto been holding them aloft.

The second type of coalescence occurs when the surrounding atmosphere is so cold that ice crystals are present with the water droplets. The two collide, with the water droplets then freezing on the crystals. The result: the crystals finally become heavy enough to fall as snow or pellets of ice. Usually they do not reach the earth as snow or ice. On passing through the warmer air near the earth's surface, they melt and change into raindrops. Only when the temperature near the earth is sufficiently cold do they fall as snow or ice.

On arriving back on earth as precipitation, the water is absorbed by—and nourishes—all the things and creatures that gave it off in the first place. Much of the water flows back into oceans, lakes, rivers, and such. Much seeps into the ground. And a major share is again transformed into water vapor by means of evapotranspiration and rises into the atmosphere as the hydrologic cycle begins anew.

Drought and the Hydrologic Cycle ○ The consequences are many when drought disrupts the hydrologic cycle. These are all the outcome of an attack on our two main supplies of fresh water: surface and groundwater.[2]

Surface water is all the fresh water that lies on the earth's surface; anything from a swamp or a river to a roadside puddle consists of surface water. Groundwater is all the fresh water that seeps into the ground and lies beneath the surface of the earth.

Of the two, groundwater is less understood by most people. On entering the ground, water sets out for the nearest ocean, with gravity pulling it downward as it travels. En route, it flows through subterranean pockets: cracks, pores, caverns, and even

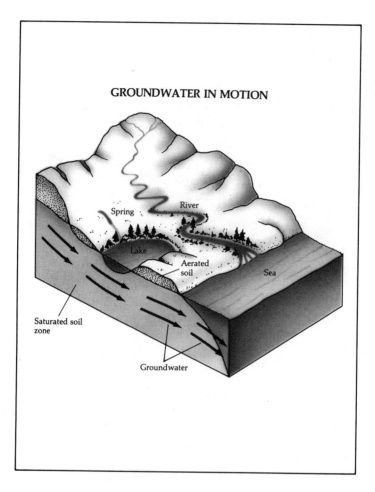

GROUNDWATER IN MOTION

Spring

River

Lake

Aerated soil

Sea

Saturated soil zone

Groundwater

Groundwater enters the topsoil as precipitation. Pulled by the force of gravity, groundwater travels downward through the saturated soil, filling up cavities along the way, which in turn replenish lakes, rivers, wells, and reservoirs. Sometimes, ground water bursts forth from breaks in the soil or rock as a spring.

porous rocks. As it passes through, some of the water becomes trapped within the pockets. Water can flow downward as far as ten miles before running into solid rock that it is unable to penetrate. A layer of groundwater lies near the surface and is called the water table.

Groundwater that becomes trapped in various subterranean pockets is especially valuable to our water supply. Spearing out from many of the pockets are channels and cracks that make their way to our sources of surface water. Groundwater works its way along these avenues and replenishes lakes, rivers, and swamps. It also feeds wells and desert oases. At some points, it surges back up to the earth's surface as springs.

Groundwater trapped in pockets offering no means of escape is also of immeasurable value. It provides the world with a vast water resource that, wherever it can be reached, can be tapped for emergencies or for irrigation, manufacture, and daily needs. Many scientists believe that as much as 97 percent of the world's fresh water supply is locked away at various depths beneath the earth's surface. (Fresh water makes up a mere 3 percent of the earth's water. The rest consists of salt water.)

Drought works its harm on our surface and ground waters by hindering one part of the hydrologic cycle while allowing the other to go on functioning. When condensation is reduced or stopped altogether, there can be no precipitation. But the cycle's evapotranspiration phase continues. It first depletes our surface water, and we make matters worse by using the remaining supply to keep on living. Plant life, requiring moisture as we do for survival, consumes its share of the surface supply. A danger is added as any river that flows into an ocean begins to run low. When a river's water level drops, salt water moves farther and farther upstream to turn the surrounding fresh water briny and dangerous to both plant and animal life.

Groundwater, too, is depleted in various ways. Without replenishment, it continues to flow from its subterranean pockets into lakes, swamps and rivers. Plants also feed on it, causing it to dwindle even further. Much of the groundwater near the surface is sacrificed to evaporation. In time, it becomes so depleted that the wells and springs it long ago created run dry.

The ocean is as much a threat to groundwater as it is to surface water. Under ordinary conditions, the fresh water beneath the earth exerts a pressure that keeps ocean water from seeping into the soil along a coastline. At work here is the fact that the groundwater, which is constantly moving towards the ocean, has at last reached the point where it is actually entering the sea; it is now pressing against the salt water with enough force to hold it in check. But, when a drought sucks up too much groundwater, it causes this pressure to drop so much that ocean water can no longer be restrained and is able to seep into the shoreside soil. One result: nearby wells fill with salty, undrinkable water. Another result: the increasing salt content in the soil damages plant roots and begins to erode farm machinery.

Types of Drought

Wherever drought strikes, it always upsets the hydrologic cycle. Though its basic effect is always the same, meteorologists have divided drought into sev-

*Alfalfa plants damaged due to high
saltwater content of the land*

eral types.[3] They have been able to do so because of ways that the world's various climates influence precipitation.

As a whole, the world receives an average of approximately 28 inches (70 cm) of rain annually. However, as everyone knows, rain does not fall in the same amount everywhere. Depending on the climate, certain regions may receive heavy, moderate, or little amounts of rain.

Tropical regions are the most heavily bathed; their atmosphere is humid, always moist and ready for condensation. Some (the Philippine Islands, for example) receive several hundred inches annually, with rainfall occurring at all times of the year. Other areas are also blessed with rainfall throughout the year, but it falls more lightly at one time than at another. Still, others receive ample rainfall, which arrives only during certain seasons, with dry conditions prevailing the rest of the time.

Other areas, such as deserts where the climate is always hot and dry (arid), receive as little as a fraction of an inch of rain per year. This can also apply to semi-arid areas, which are dry for much of the year but receive a light rainfall at certain times.

Though drought works in the same manner worldwide, its nature is determined by the climate* of the area under attack. There are four types of drought: permanent, contingent, seasonal, and invisible.

---

* The term *climate* should not be confused with the word *weather*. *Weather* describes the momentary or day-to-day actions of the atmosphere at any point in the world, such as a sudden rain or a passing warm spell. *Climate*, which is often called "historical weather," refers to the general type of weather experienced in an area year after year.

Permanent Drought ○ Permanent drought, as its name indicates, persists all year round. It is found in regions with dry and hot climates that permit evapotranspiration to take place but do not provide the upper-elevation coolness necessary for condensation and precipitation.

Technically, it is not quite correct to list permanent drought as a type of drought. Unlike its counterparts, it does not fit the definitions given for drought.

You'll recall that drought is defined as a "prolonged period" of dry weather; the word *period* indicates that droughts come and go. Permanent drought does not. It is present at all times. For this reason, meteorologists look on it not as a type of drought but as the outcome of climatic conditions that provide a region with so few and such meager rains that it is rendered perennially arid and unable to maintain all but a few hardy plants. The result is that drought conditions are a way of life there.

In the next chapter, we'll look at the climatic conditions that cause this problem. But for now, let us just say that the world's deserts—from the Sahara in Africa and the Gobi Desert in the Orient to the desert region of northern Chile and the great desert of the U.S. southwest—are the locales of permanent drought. In general, an area receiving less than 6 to 10 inches (15 to 25 cm) of rain per year is classed as a desert.

We usually think of deserts as places of great heat. But there is another kind of desert that also produces conditions of permanent drought. Found in the north and south polar regions (and also in Soviet Union's Siberia), it suffers temperatures so low at ground level and in the higher elevations that they disrupt all phases of the hydrologic cycle, with the result that scant rain is produced and practically no form of plant life can survive.

Contingent Drought ○ Contingent drought occurs in areas that do not have an especially heavy rainfall annually, but do have rain that is adequate enough for life. This drought occurs when some misbehavior on the weather's part causes a drop in the normal amount of precipitation. It may arrive at any time of the year, may be of any intensity, and may stay a short or long while.

Semi-arid regions are usually the victims of contingent drought. An area is classed as semi-arid when it receives up to 15 inches (37.5 cm) of rainfall a year.

The world's major semi-arid regions are made up of vast stretches of flat and rolling grasslands. Known as steppes or prairies, they are found in the Soviet Union, western and southern Africa, Brazil, Australia, India, and the United States. These regions are particularly vulnerable to the harsh winds that often accompany drought because they are generally treeless and thus have no means of breaking or slowing the wind's force. All are located close to desert areas. The Great Plains, which spread out from the deserts of our southwest, are America's prairie lands.

A North Dakota farmer examines his dry wheat crop.

Prairie lands serve as the world's principal providers of wheat, corn, and other grains. They have the ideal soil content and climate for grain—light nourishing rains during the growing season (late spring and early summer) and dry, sunny weather during the ripening and harvesting season (late summer).

Seasonal Drought ○ Seasonal drought occurs in areas where there are distinct and regular wet and dry seasons, with the dry seasons being the time when drought is most likely to occur. In such areas, plants either die or remain dormant during the dry season. Farming in such areas must be carried on with irrigation during the dry season or must wait until the rainy season arrives.

Invisible Drought ○ Invisible drought strikes in regions where rain is a possibility at any time of the year. It occurs when there is some moisture in the atmosphere to feed the local plant life, but not enough to replace all that is being sent aloft by evapotranspiration. Usually arriving in the summertime, it is called "invisible" because it gives little warning of its presence. Plants look healthy and normal. There may even be some showers to delude everyone into thinking that everything is as it should be.

A farmer (or an alert backyard gardener) will begin to suspect an invisible drought when the leaves and stalks of growing plants, while appearing to be in good health, may be drier than usual. Suspicions will be replaced by certainty at harvest time. Crops are likely to be smaller and far less abundant than in a drought-free year. For example, let's say a farm produces about eight tons (7.3 metric tons) of a certain crop in a normal year. As the victim of invisible drought, the crop will be down to between, say, six and seven tons (5.4 to 6.3 metric tons).

Now that we've met the enemy and seen it at work in its various forms, it's time to turn to the factors that cause drought to strike throughout the world.

CHAPTER THREE

———○———

WHY DROUGHT STRIKES

The causes of drought are many and complex. Some are so complex and mysterious that they are not fully understood by today's meteorologists, even though we live in a time of extensive scientific knowledge and research. But one thing is certain: drought is triggered by the behavior and interaction of various forces in nature. These are forces that range from the wind and the sun's heat to the different air pressures found in the atmosphere and the sunspots seen some 93 million miles (149 million km) out in space.

Wind and Drought

The wind can bring on droughts by altering its force or shifting its direction. We can see each of these actions in turn by looking at two widely separated regions: the United States and southern Asia.

A Change in Force ○ Most of the United States lies within the latitudinal zone where the prevailing winds are called the westerlies.[1] The zone stretches between 30 degrees and 60 degrees north latitude. This means that our winds, though they can blow in any direction at times, come mainly from some point in the west and blow eastward. Specifically, the westerlies blow along an oblique path than can come from slightly south of west all the way up to slightly north of west. The path chosen by the winds depends on the season of the year. All winds are named for the direction from which they blow and not the direction in which they are traveling. Northerly winds, for example, come from the north, and southerly winds from the south.

Located immediately to our south is another latitudinal zone. The northeasterly direction from which the prevailing winds in this zone blow gave them their name—the trade winds. Captains of early merchant ships bound from Europe to trade with the New World found that, once caught in the northeasterly winds, their vessels were carried quickly to ports in the Caribbean and along the South American coast. Florida and the coastlines of the states bordering on the Gulf of Mexico lie within this zone, which extends from 30 degrees north latitude south to 10 degrees north latitude. Some of the wind makes its way north and enters the zone of the westerlies.

Our westerlies and the winds moving north from our neighboring zone combine to have an effect on the states of the American Great Plains. They either enrich the agricultural production of these states or plague them with drought. Here is what happens.

The winds arriving from the south are warm and moist. They carry water evaporated from the Caribbean Sea. As they move northward, they encounter the westerlies. If all is well—if the westerlies are blowing with their customary vigor—they catch the southerly winds, cool them, and nudge them eastward across the Plains states. Cooling, the southerlies condense their moisture content and release it to enrich the farmlands of the nation's "bread basket."

But in a year—or a span of years—when the westerlies fail to blow with their usual force, the moisture-laden southerly winds make their way farther north before the westerlies manage to push them eastward. Rain falls to the north of the Plains states, and the Plains states themselves are gripped by drought.

A Shift in Direction ○ Various lands to either side of the equator—usually lying within 20 latitudinal degrees north and south of the equator—are subject to *monsoons.*[2] Among the regions visited by the monsoons are southeastern Asia, India, and parts of Africa, South America, Australia, and even the southwestern United States.

Monsoons are winds that blow from one direction for part of the year and then swing about to flow in from another direction for the rest of the year. Their name comes from the Arabic word *mausim,* which means *seasonal.*

The effects of the monsoons on certain areas in southeast Asia and India are especially dramatic. The winds come from the northeast for half of every year—during the autumn and winter months— bringing with them cool and dry weather. For the other half of the year, they turn about and blow from the south. On making an about-face, they carry moist air in from the Indian Ocean and release it as rain. In many areas, the rain is torrential; the downpour in parts of India comes to more than 80 inches (200 cm).* Other areas are more lightly touched, but still receive an ample rainfall: 25 inches (62.5 cm) or more. The monsoon rains provide the water that people need for survival during all the months when the winds will again bring dry weather from the north.

Though monsoons are most dramatically seen in southeast Asia and India, monsoonlike winds also strike Japan, eastern and central China, and the southeastern United States. Unlike the classic monsoons, these winds can bring rain all year round—in amounts up to 40 to 80 inches (100 to 200 cm) annually. But the rain, like that of the classic monsoons, is distinctly heavier during the summer months.

As long as monsoons blow steadily from the south, the lands in their path are drenched with welcome rain. But, on occasion, atmospheric conditions create a westerly wind that strikes the monsoons and pushes them off course, directing them eastward. Their rains end up back where they started—in the Indian Ocean—and miss the lands that need them so. The result: a seasonal drought that affects millions of people.

The Sahel region of Africa is an area that depends on monsoons from the South Atlantic for its rainfall. Sahel's terrible drought of 1968 to 1974, which claimed more than 100,000 lives, was caused by winds that shifted the rain-laden monsoon air so that it bypassed Sahel to the south.

---

* Because its rain is so torrential, many people think a monsoon is a rainstorm rather than a wind. While the terms are used interchangeably, remember the monsoon is a wind, not the rain it brings.

Atmospheric Pressure
and Drought

Invisible though it is, air has weight. This weight is expressed in the pressure that air exerts on its surroundings. The atmosphere is marked by masses (called cells) of high-pressure and low-pressure air.[3] The air in a high-pressure cell is cool, dense, and heavy. Conversely, the air in a low-pressure cell is warm, moist, and light. Meteorologists refer to the cells simply as *highs* and *lows*.

In many areas, the highs and lows almost routinely trade places. These trades play a major role in creating changes in weather. A high customarily brings dry weather. A low can bring anything from unsettled to stormy weather.

High-Pressure Air and Permanent Drought ○ While the cells routinely change places in many areas, there are some regions where highs are almost always on hand. Called permanent highs, they are almost always present above the world's major deserts, such as north Africa's Sahara and Chile's great northern desert.* They are responsible for the arid climate that gives the deserts the conditions needed for permanent drought.

What happens here is that high-pressure air forces itself downward to the earth's surface. As it does so, it is heated by both the sun and the warmth that the earth has absorbed from the sun and is radiating back into the atmosphere. It is further heated by the fact that air above it is pushing down-

---

* The lowest annual rainfall in the world is recorded in one section of the Chilean desert: 0.02 inches (0.05 cm).

ward and compressing it. A fiery heat is generated that keeps the water vapor in the air from cooling, condensing, and falling as precipitation. At those times when rain does manage to fall, its amount is usually negligible. Areas classed as deserts receive only a fraction of an inch to between 6 and 10 inches (15 to 25 cm) of rainfall annually.

High-pressure air also descends and is greatly compressed in the polar regions, turning them into areas of permanent drought conditions. But because of the earth's tilt these regions are not as directly exposed to the sun as are the earth's hottest spots. And so there is not the stunning heat that prevents condensation and precipitation in a desert. Rather, the air in polar regions is rendered too cold to support plant life.

Permanent Ocean Highs and Drought ○ There are permanent highs over two of the world's major oceans, the Atlantic and the Pacific. The larger of the two hangs above the Atlantic, stretching across the ocean from Spain and the western regions of Africa to the southeast United States. The Pacific high is situated a distance off the California coast. Both can produce drought conditions in the United States.

Both highs are smaller in the winter than in the summer. When the Pacific high expands in the summer months, it spreads itself up the western face of the United States to the northwestern states and threatens drought conditions all along the coast; the threat can be carried far inland when the high is strongly expanded. As for the Atlantic high, its expansion brings winds that, inhibiting condensation, can lead to drought conditions along the Atlantic seaboard.

Highs and Other Droughts ○ A high-pressure cell can also generate contingent, seasonal, and invisible droughts. This usually happens when atmospheric conditions cause a high to become "stalled" over an area. Once stalled, it can remain in place for days and even weeks. Its presence prevents a low from coming in to replace it and feed the earth with rain. In general, lows always follow highs to provide a balance in weather conditions.

Actually, a stalled high can do two types of harm. If it arrives and lingers over an area where rain is either expected or needed, it can, of course, quickly produce drought conditions. But suppose a high is hanging stubbornly over a broad region and is preventing a low from moving in from a neighboring area miles away. The area blanketed by the low is an agricultural one whose young crop plantings do not require a great deal of water at the time. A situation exactly opposite drought, but potentially just as dangerous, is in the making. Blocked as it is, the low may release rain that damages or ruins the crops. Everyone—from farmer to consumer—may end up suffering the very same problems that a drought brings.

Land, Sea, and Drought

By combining forces, the world's lands and seas are able to generate conditions that can result in drought.[4] This happens because the land and sea do not absorb and release the sun's heat at the same rate of speed.

The land absorbs heat, much faster than the ocean. It does so because the heat can penetrate the thick soil to a depth of just a few inches. A major share of the heat remains on the surface, and the heat that has penetrated the soil to such a shallow depth is quickly radiated back out. For this reason, the land at night continues to release its heat quickly.

As for ocean water, the sun's heat can penetrate it to a depth of 80 feet (24 m) or more. Further, the heat collects slowly because the ocean is being constantly stirred by winds and currents, causing the colder water far below the surface to mingle with the warmer water near the surface. Consequently, an ocean radiates its warmth slowly, with the slowness continuing into the night. Thus, the air above the ocean is cooler than land air in the daytime, and warmer than land air at night.

These differing cooling speeds make an ocean colder than the land in the summer and warmer in the winter. They cause the interiors of continents to have colder winters and hotter summers than do coastal areas and islands, with the summer heat often creating drought conditions.

But the coastal regions are not altogether safe from drought. In the winter, when the warmer, moisture-laden ocean air sweeps in over the cooler coastal land, its moisture content condenses and falls as rain or snow. But, in the summer, when the land air is hotter and drier, the moisture carried in from the sea is evaporated and precipitation is either reduced or lost altogether.

Land Contours ○ The characteristics of the land help to induce drought conditions. At work here are the shapes, or contours, of land in a given area. Depending on the length and breadth of the contours, drought conditions may be limited to a small area or extend over a broad region.

An example of what the shape of the land does to an extensive region can be seen by looking at the Sierra Nevada mountains, which lie in the path of the winds moving across California from the Pacific. The Sierras are rich in vegetation on their windward (western) side, but dry and able to boast only sparse vegetation on their leeward (eastern) side.* What happens here is that the Pacific air is heated as it passes over the relatively warmer land. On encountering the Sierras, it moves up the mountainsides and cools as it travels higher and higher, until it is able to condense and form clouds that release their moisture as rain or snow on the western slopes and at the summits. Once it clears the summits, the air starts down the eastern slopes. Descending, it is warmed. As usual, the clouds evaporate. There is little precipitation, causing the land below to be dry and less fertile.

If we turn from the mountains and look to a desert area, we'll find that the topography there helps to fashion the conditions of permanent drought. Deserts are customarily found in basins— low lying areas of varying size that are surrounded by hills or mountains. The surrounding hills keep the high-pressure air locked within the basin and thus help to intensify the heating that, in turn, intensifies evaporation and hinders precipitation.

Ocean Currents ○ Ocean currents also play a role in generating drought. Some flow away from the polar regions and carry cold water toward the equator. Those that pass close to the edges of continents cre-

---

* The term *windward* means in the path of the wind. *Leeward* means away from or out of the wind.

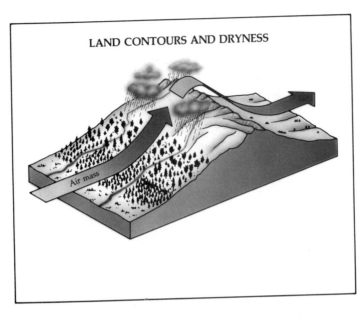

LAND CONTOURS AND DRYNESS

The rich variety of trees on the windward side of this mountain range forms bands that force the warm, moist air to rise over the mountain barrier. Here, water vapor condenses into clouds, which rain or snow on the mountain peaks. Once over the barrier (having released most of its moisture), the air descends the leeward side of the range with fewer and fewer clouds, leaving behind a dry zone.

ate drought conditions by chilling the winds blowing above them. As the winds sweep ashore, their temperatures are suddenly and dramatically thrust upward by the heat emanating from the land. The result, as always, is increased evaporation and the loss of the condensation necessary for precipitation.

Cold ocean currents are especially strong along the coasts of Peru and northern Chile, both of which have broad desert areas. The cold water causes Peru to receive little precipitation other than a light drizzle. However, at times when the cold water current is replaced by warmer water, the outcome for both Peru and Chile is the exact opposite of drought. There are torrential rains that can be as disastrous as a drought.

Strong cold ocean currents are also found off the Atlantic coasts of southwest and northwest Africa. Located in the southwest is the sprawling Kalahari Desert. The regions of the Sahara Desert known as the Moroccan Sahara and Spanish Sahara lie in northwest Africa. Both areas are noted for their dry conditions.

The many forces that, singly or in combination, cause drought must now be joined by another factor. Though drought can strike at any time, there has long been the question of whether it has the tendency to run in cycles—that is, to occur at regular or irregular intervals.

CHAPTER FOUR

———○———

DROUGHT
IN CYCLES

Do droughts come in cycles?

For some types of drought, the answer, perhaps first voiced by the world's earliest farmers, is "yes." Knowing how much their crops—and, hence, their very lives—were at the mercy of the weather, farmers kept a sharp eye out for rainy and dry conditions. In time, experience taught them that drought would often appear at fairly regular intervals. In the centuries since, weather scientists have amassed much evidence to support what daily watchfulness had shown the early farmers.

The evidence has come from many sources.[1] For one, there have been studies made of ancient pollens found in the soil and in the beds of rivers and lakes; changes noted in their natures and structures have indicated periodic onslaughts by drought. For another, research into early animal and human migrations have unearthed patterns that indicate the need to find water and new fertile ground at intervals. One of the most fruitful sources has been the study of the internal rings that mark the growth of trees.

The Evidence: Tree Rings

The study of tree rings* has proved to be not only a fine source of evidence but an especially fascinating one as well.[2] Each year of its life, a tree girdles itself with a new layer of wood. These layers appear as rings when the tree is cut and viewed in cross-section. They are superb indicators of past weather because the layers that took shape during years of ample rain are always thicker than those that formed in years of little or no rain. Depending on the life spans of different species of trees, the rings can be used to track a region's weather conditions, including the occurrence of drought, back over several hundred to a thousand or more years—even farther back in the case of redwoods and bristlecone pines. Redwoods are capable of living for 2,000 years. Some bristlecone pines are over 4,600 years old. They are believed to be the oldest living things on the planet. In the western and midwestern United States, the chronologies of trees, and the weather patterns they reveal, have been traced back more than 8,000 years by studying both living and dead trees.

By studying the number of thinner rings and the spacings in between, scientists can determine whether drought has visited an area randomly or at somewhat regular intervals in the past. Studies of the rings—and of other evidence, such as the ancient pollens—have shown that drought often tends to come in cycles, arriving in some areas, for in-

---

* The science of studying tree rings and allied subjects is called *dendrochronology*. The term comes from the Greek words *dendron*, meaning "tree" and *chronos* meaning "time."

stance, about every seven years and in others every thirty-five years or so. Drought has struck the western and midwestern plains of the United States at twenty- to twenty-two-year intervals; the Sahel region of Africa suffers drought at the same intervals. On average, drought hits the lower region of the Yellow River in China every nine to ten years.

But one point must always be kept in mind whenever there is any talk of drought working in cycles. Drought follows no rules. It can—and does—occur at any time, striking lightly or severely, and remaining for a long or short duration. This means that it can crop up in any degree at any time between its expected appearances. And, when one of its cycles is due, it is quite capable of arriving before or later than expected. All these characteristics make it exceedingly difficult, if not impossible, for anyone to predict drought's cyclical arrival, its severity, and the length of its stay.

The Causes of Cyclical Drought

What causes some droughts to be cyclical?

Since drought is the result of myriad complex forces, scientists readily admit that they are far from knowing all the answers to this question. But they are observing two phenomena as possible major causes. At the moment, they can only suspect the first. They are pretty certain, however, that the second plays a vital role in generating cyclical drought.

The first possible cause involves what are called sunspots—phenomena that appear on the sun some 93 million miles out in space. The second involves the waters of the Pacific Ocean.

Sunspots are dark spots or blotches that break out on the face of the sun. Their cause is not known for certain, but they are understood to be made up of gases that are associated with strong electromagnetic activity on the sun.[3] Visible from the earth, they change in number from year to year and vary in size. On average, however, they measure 25,000 miles (40,000 km) in diameter.

Sunspots have long been known to scientists here on earth. They were seen by the ancient Greeks. Some fifteen centuries ago, Chinese astronomers sighted an especially large sunspot. The Italian mathematical physicist Galileo (1564–1642) is credited with being one of the first men to view sunspots through a telescope. Their activity has been tracked ever since his time.

Sunspot Cycles ○ Centuries of sunspot observation have shown that they appear in cycles. Each cycle lasts approximately eleven years. Each begins with the sun relatively unmarked by the blotches, after which the spots grow in number for a time and then begin to disappear. At the end of the eleven-year period, the sun is once again free of them.

Today, many scientists strongly feel that the activity of the sunspots is connected with many climatic behaviors. For instance, the centuries of sunspot tracking have revealed that their numbers are apt to vary from cycle to cycle or over a string of cycles. For extended periods, the number in the cycles will be small, while at other times it will be great. During those periods when the number is on the small side,

Dark spots, called sunspots, break out in the surface of the sun. Scientists speculate that sunspot cycles affect the earth's climate.

the general temperature on earth is cooler. It is warmer when the number is higher than usual.

In addition, there is a growing suspicion that the sunspot cycle may be connected with an increase in United States tornado activity and with the cyclical appearance of drought. The suspicion of a tornado-sunspot connection has come about because the United States experiences a higher frequency of the deadly storms roughly every forty-five years—approximately four sunspot cycles.

Sunspots and Drought ○ As for a connection between sunspot cycles and cyclical drought, the suspicion here rises from a number of studies. One study had to do with tree rings and was of particular importance to Americans. It was conducted by scientists with the University of Arizona Tree Ring Laboratory and the National Oceanic and Atmospheric Administration. It began with the long-held knowledge that drought tends to strike the plains of the American west and midwest every twenty to twenty-two years. The scientists realized that this drought cycle coincided approximately with two sunspot cycles. They wondered if this was coincidence or if the drought and sunspot cycles matched in some way.

To see if there is actually a connection, the scientists studied the rings of trees growing at sixty sites in the western half of the nation. The study, aided by computers, led to the finding that summer droughts tend to occur every twenty to twenty-two years at times when the sunspots are at a minimum during every other sunspot cycle. The scientists were able to trace the pattern back to the 1600s.

But, as indicative of a sunspot-drought connection as it was, the finding left the scientists with no more than a strong suspicion of the link. They could not be absolutely certain of the link because the study also produced a number of puzzling, seemingly contradictory points. A principal one was the fact that the drought cycle exactly matched the twenty-two-year double sunspot cycle in only 25 percent of the cases; the rest of the time, it missed the mark altogether or only came close. Nevertheless, the suspicion was strong enough for scientists to continue investigating a possible link between the two cycles. Perhaps future research will reveal such a link.

Warm and Cold Pacific Waters

Recently, scientists have come to suspect that the single most important cause of drought in the world is a sea-air phenomenon. It involves, first, a stretch of the Pacific Ocean at the equator and, second, bands of wind far away to the north and south. To see it in action, we need to know the meaning of three terms—*jet stream*, *El Niño*, and *La Niña*.

Jet Streams ○ Jet streams are bands of high-speed winds that are found about 6 miles above the earth.[4] They flow at such an extreme height that their presence was not detected until World War II, when they were first encountered by high-altitude aircraft. The jet streams are narrow, usually no more than a few hundred miles wide, but they can extend more than halfway around the world. Their winds blow at various speeds—anywhere from 67 to 335 miles an hour (107 to 536 km per hour).

Of the several such wind bands high in the atmosphere, two exert the most influence on the world's weather—one in the northern hemisphere, the other in the southern. Each is located at about 50 degrees latitude, which means that the band in the northern hemisphere passes across the United States. Both streams flow from west to east. They do not, however, travel in a straight line, but dance about to form curves, arcs, and loops.

The flow of the two major jet streams and their various "dances" control the development and movement of the high- and low-pressure cells that produce our weather. For example, when a jet stream describes deep curves as it flows along, it slows its speed and creates the atmospheric conditions that enable highs to become "stalled" for days or weeks at a time and quickly induce drought conditions. The jet streams are also responsible for creating the atmospheric conditions that give Asia and other parts of the world their monsoons and monsoon rains.

El Niño and La Niña ○ *El Niño* and *La Niña* are the names given to two different massive strips of water—one exceptionally warm and the other abnormally cold—that take shape in the Pacific Ocean and stretch westward along the equator from a point near South America.[5] They do not occur side by side in the ocean but periodically exchange places. Each exchange creates a major upheaval in the world's weather.

El Niño is the band of exceptionally warm water. In Spanish, the term means "boy." Peruvians call it the Christ Child because it customarily appears off their coast during the Christmas season. It is often described as a heat wave at sea.

La Niña is its opposite—the strip of especially cold water. The term is Spanish for "girl." Some scientists consider this name to be sexist and have replaced it with *El Viejo,* meaning "old man." Many South Americans think of the cold water band as Old Man Winter because, like El Niño, it begins to take shape in the winter. Most scientists have sidestepped the three names by simply referring to the comings and goings of El Niño and La Niña as cold and warm events, or cycles.

Each coming-and-going lasts about two years. For some unknown reason, however, El Niño does not always replace La Niña at the end of every two-year period. Sometimes, it waits as long as ten years before putting in an appearance.

When one or the other appears on the scene, it has far-reaching consequences. The warm-water El Niño reshapes the weather along the American coast of the Pacific, dumping torrential rains all along the South American coast and whipping the southern U.S. coast with hurricanes; at the same time, it triggers droughts elsewhere in the world. But, when La Niña appears, the cold water brings drought to the United States and disastrous rain to the Asian countries clear across the Pacific.

Scientists have yet to understand fully the forces that bring El Niño and La Niña to life. But they do know what forces go to work once one or the other takes shape. We can see those forces in the story of La Niña's appearance in 1988 and how it reached far out to generate drought in the United States and killer rains in Asia.

1988: La Niña Strikes ○ Actually, La Niña began to form in 1987. Over a period of months, it pushed the warm water at the equator northward and westward. The northward-moving water entered what is called the intertropical convergence zone, a region where rains and thunderstorms are commonplace because of the way the winds meet and clash. On arrival there, La Niña created atmospheric conditions that began moving the zone northward; at the same time, for a reason yet unknown, a mass of warm water appeared near Hawaii. Soon, the zone moved into this warm-water mass, with the result that a number of thunderstorms broke out. They created a series of high- and low-pressure cells over a wide area north of Hawaii.

These cells exerted an effect on the northern hemisphere's jet stream—an effect that ended in drought in the United States. They caused the jet stream to begin traveling in deep curves. As it traveled above the United States, the stream curved far to the north. Because it reduces its speed eastward during a curve, the stream created a "stalled" high-pressure area over much of the country and brought on long weeks of drought.

The United States was not alone in experiencing the drought induced by La Niña. Peru and Chile also suffered. La Niña intensified the chill in the cold water current off their shores, resulting in drier coastal areas.

But what of the killer rains? How did they come about? At fault here was the warm equatorial water that La Niña pushed not to the north but to the west. It began "piling up" off the Asian coast, adding its moisture-laden air to the damp monsoons blowing in from the Indian and Pacific Oceans. As a consequence, the monsoon rains were heavier than usual and brought heavy flooding to a number of areas.

GLOBAL WEATHER ACTIONS CAUSED BY LA NIÑA (1989)

This figure illustrates a theory that links global weather connections with drought.

According to the theory, a 1988 drought in the United States can be traced to periodic shifts in winds and ocean temperatures in the tropical Pacific. Unusually cold water along the equator (1) pushed the intertropical convergence zone upward (2), where tradewinds collided farther north than usual. Unusually warm water southeast of Hawaii also pulled the zone northward. The zone clashed with the warm water (3), resulting in a series of thunderstorms (4). The storms disrupted the atmosphere (5), triggering ripples and swirls, which turned into high- and low-pressure systems. These pushed the jet stream far north (6), creating a large, rainless high-pressure system (7), which brought on weeks of drought.

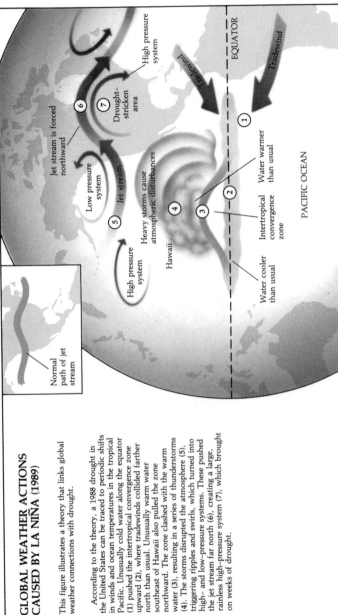

Normal path of jet stream

High pressure system

EQUATOR

Tradewind

Tradewind

① Water warmer than usual

PACIFIC OCEAN

Drought-stricken area

⑦

⑥ Jet stream is forced northward

Low pressure system

⑤ Jet stream

Heavy storms cause atmospheric disturbances

② Intertropical convergence zone

③

④

High pressure system

Hawaii

Water cooler than usual

Especially hard hit was the nation of Bangladesh, which lies to the east of India. The flooding there took at least 1,000 lives.

The far-flung harm that El Niño can do can be seen by looking at one of its most powerful appearances in recent times. The year was 1983.

1983: El Niño Strikes ○ The story opens in 1982, when the warm water that had been "piled up" along the Asian coast by a preceding La Niña began to flow back across the Pacific toward South America. Penetrating to a depth of 450 feet (135 m) or more, and keeping the cold water deep in the ocean from rising to the surface, the warm water spread out over half the equatorial Pacific. It finally lay still and hot near the South American coast—so hot that, at points, the surface temperature exceeded 80°F (27°C), as much as fifteen or more degrees above normal.

The consequences were devastating for the countries of Peru, Chile, Bolivia, Ecuador, and Brazil. For example, when moist, hot water replaced the cold-water current that gives Peru and Chile their dry climates, the two countries were struck by monstrous downpours. Some desert regions recorded from 12 to 15 feet (3.6 to 4.5 m) of rain that loosed flash floods and mudslides. Hundreds of people lost their lives and thousands fled their homes in the face of the deluge. Offshore, the hot water either killed or drove away sea life along the Pacific coast. Among the fish lost were anchovies, a mainstay of the Peruvian economy.

Meantime, severe storms battered the Pacific coast of the United States and, far to the east, Florida. They did an estimated $1 billion in damage and took the lives of more than 100 people. As in South

America, the fishing industry all along the west coast, from southern California to northern Washington, suffered when the warm seas sent the albacore and salmon in search of colder waters. Far out in the Pacific, a string of typhoons lashed the island of Tahiti. The island had not yet experienced a single typhoon in this century.

And there was drought. It spread over a vast area. Atmospheric disturbances generated droughts in Australia, Indonesia, India, Sri Lanka, and southern Africa in 1983. In February of the year, an Australian dust storm blanketed the city of Melbourne with thousands of tons of dirt.

While scientists are not yet certain of the forces that cause La Niña and El Niño, they are aware of a phenomenon that accompanies them and may well play some role in triggering their appearances. El Niño and La Niña both operate near and in the latitudinal band of the trade winds. The winds are always brisk when La Niña takes shape, and always weak—even dead—when El Niño steps forward. But are these differences in wind velocity responsible for the appearances of the bands of water or do they simply help them do their work once they are on the scene? For example, do the deadened winds allow El Niño to move its warm water back across the Pacific from Asia to South America? Or does the warm water create atmospheric conditions that deaden the winds?

These questions—and many others—remain to be answered before we have a full understanding of why El Niño and La Niña come into being and how they operate. Once the answers are finally learned, scientists may at last know for certain what many of their number now strongly suspect—that El Niño and La Niña stand together as the single most important cause of drought (and other weather upheavals) in the world. And weather services may finally be able to predict accurately the arrivals of the two and enable us to be better prepared to defend ourselves against them and the widespread destruction they can bring.

CHAPTER FIVE

———○———

UNENDING ATTACKS

Drought has been with us ever since the atmosphere formed around our planet millions of years ago and gave birth to the weather. But until humans learned to write, droughts went unrecorded (except for a few that were related in the folk tales that early peoples passed from one generation to another). Even after writing was devised, many droughts continued to go unrecorded. Some were of so little consequence that they were not thought worth reporting. Many others—some of which were of awesome magnitude—occurred in such remote regions that news of them never reached the rest of the world.

Despite these facts, people have been able to build a pretty detailed picture of drought's age-old presence in the world. Findings revealed by such sciences* as archaeology, botany, climatology, pale-

* Archaeology is the study of the material remains of past human life, activities, and cultures; botany is the study of plant life; climatology is the study of past and present climates and their associated phenomena; paleontology is the study of life in past geological periods as revealed by fossil remains; dendrochronology is the study of tree life.

ontology, and dendrochronology have taught us much about the droughts that struck long before there was such a thing as the written word. The history has been rounded out by eye-witness reports and accounts of droughts in more recent times. Altogether, it is an ugly picture of unending onslaughts and widespread hardship and death.

Every part of the world—every continent (Even Antarctica, which is considered to be a type of desert and thus endures the conditions of permanent drought.)—has been attacked.[1] For example:

Europe: There is evidence that drought conditions existed in what are today's Sweden and England in the 24th to the 22nd centuries B.C., and that they spread into western Europe in the 23rd century B.C. and remained there for some 200 years.

Africa: From ancient Egypt come records of the drought and famine that struck when the Nile River—the water source that made farming, commerce, and life possible there—ran dry or suffered a drop in its level because of sparse rains in the lands far to the south where it takes shape.

Asia: The newspapers of the day reported that drought and the famine it brought took the lives of approximately 9.5 million people in northern China in 1877 and 1878. China has suffered a long history of drought, caused by the periodic failure of the monsoon rains on which the nation depends for its water.

The Americas: The British naturalist Charles Darwin, during his famous research trip around the world aboard the H.M.S. *Beagle* in the last century, reported a catastrophic drought in South America. It lasted from from 1827 to 1830.

It is impossible to mention in one chapter, or even one book, all the droughts that have struck the world since the dawn of time. But a well-rounded picture of what drought has done through the centuries can be shown by the stories of how it has attacked three widely separated areas.

India

India has always been vulnerable to droughts because it depends on the annual monsoon rains for its water. When they fail to arrive, the country faces disaster. India's history of drought can be traced back to an ancient and vanished people.

The Death of the Harappan Civilization ○ More than 5,000 years ago, one of the world's first great civilizations flourished in the Indus River Valley.[2] Known as the Harappan civilization, its domain stretched across a quarter of a million square miles (650,000 sq km) of present-day Pakistan and northern India. It consisted of fine farms and more than 100 cities and towns. The region was crisscrossed by canals for the transportation of goods between the farms and cities. The cities, mainly of brick, boasted such features as heated public baths, indoor plumbing, and underground sewage systems. The people knew how to read, write, and compute.

Sometime between 1800 and 1700 B.C., the Harappan civilization began to disappear. In time, it vanished altogether. Dust replaced the region's fine soil, eventually burying the cities so completely that they were not seen again until an archaeological team stumbled upon one of these cities in 1922. Ever since that discovery, the question of what befell the Harappan people and caused the death of their civilization has puzzled scientists and historians. They have come up with a number of theories.

One theory holds that the Harappans were the victims of catastrophic floods or earthquakes. Another is that they suffered some terrible economic or political upheaval. Still another (it is widely doubted) contends that they were overrun and slaughtered or driven off by a horde of brutal invaders who swept through the Himalaya Mountains and into India from central Asia.

A recent investigation of the bed of a 10,000-year-old lake in the Harappan region has added another possibility to the list. It indicates that these ancient people fell victim to a prolonged drought—a drought that lasted for an incredible 700 years.

Was Drought the Killer? ○ The study centered on the pollens of various plants that grew in the lake in ancient times. The lake today is a salt lake, but the pollens unearthed at certain levels in its bed show that it was once made up of fresh water; they reveal the characteristics of freshwater plants. However, pollens found at other levels of the lake bed show that a change disastrous for the Harappans began to take place 3,600 years ago. The pollens found at these levels show the characteristics of saltwater plants. Such a change indicates the presence of drought because the salts in the air and ground accumulate on the earth's surface when there is not enough rain to wash them away.

The study also indicates that the lake received at least three times more rain prior to 3,600 years ago than it does at present. During those years of ample rain, the study adds, the Harappans did an excellent job of building waterways and draining away excess water. But they did not concentrate on storing water so that it could be used to irrigate their fields in times of need. Rather, they put their faith in the monsoon rains, trusting them to arrive each year and provide the fields with all the water that was required. Then came those terrible 700 years when, because of some atmospheric change or upheaval, the rains too often failed to arrive—and a civilization vanished.

Two Killer Droughts ○ If indeed drought did strike the Harappans, it is memorable for the length of its stay and the fact that it destroyed a civilization. But droughts of shorter duration in India have been just as memorable for the number of lives they have claimed. The point can be proved with just two examples, one from the seventeenth century and the other from the nineteenth century:

> *1769–70:* The monsoons fail to bring rain and, in a period of twenty-four months, an estimated 10 million people lose their lives as a result of the famine that follows widespread crop failures. Millions are uprooted from their homes and wander the countryside in search of food and water. Disease stalks the land with them. Smallpox and starvation are major causes of death.

1865–66: Again, the monsoon rains fail and, again, an estimated 10 million lose their lives. The situation is all the more tragic because there is ample grain in storage, but it is withheld from those most in need of it—the poor—when the British, who control the country, decide that it should be placed on sale rather than handed out to the people.

Greedy Indian merchants worsen matters by hoarding supplies of grain and then selling it at outrageously high prices. Consequently, only the wealthy in a country of widespread poverty are able to fill their bellies. Millions of their fellow countrymen die of starvation. By 1867, the situation is so desperate that the British authorities change their minds and begin to ship free rice to the areas hardest hit by the drought. But the monsoon rains come with a vengeance that year, flooding and damaging the roads so that the desperately needed shipments cannot reach their destinations.

The Sahara Desert

Many scientists believe that the vast Sahara Desert was once a region blessed by rain throughout the year.[3] This belief is based on various findings, among them fossilized bits of ancient plant and animal life. All suggest that what is now the world's largest desert—it covers some 3.5 million square miles (9.1 million sq km) in northern Africa—was once a highly fertile area.

*A portion of the great
Sahara Desert, in Algeria*

Further, there remains today some very obvious evidence of a long-ago fertility. The Sahara is marked here and there with spots of dense vegetation and high and stable water tables. Called oases, these spots provide water all year long and enable the growth of such plant life as date trees. Such signs of an ancient fertility are also found in some other desert regions of the world.

How the Sahara was transformed into a desert is a mystery. Did the world's climate change at some point in the distant past and create the conditions of unending dryness? Or did other factors play a part in the transformation?

Climatic Changes ○ The answer to both questions may be "yes." There have been climatic changes throughout the long history of the world and there is no reason to believe that some did not affect the great desert areas. It should be noted that, in general, the Sahara and the world's other major deserts are grouped together in two broad latitudinal bands that circle the globe. They all lie to either side of the equator, between 15 degrees and 40 degrees north and south latitudes. Is it possible that the deserts along these lines were, like the Sahara, fertile at one time and then changed to what they are today because of some momentous atmospheric upheaval?*

* The two bands are fed by the trade winds. The conditions of permanent drought seen in desert areas are created by the way in which the trade winds clash. The clash generates the high-pressure cells that force cool air downward to be heated and compressed to the point where evaporation becomes so great that condensation cannot take place and produce precipitation. While high-pressure cells switch places with low-pressure cells in most parts of the world, they are almost always present above desert areas.

Located within the band to the north of the equator are the Sahara, the Arabian desert, the Indian Desert of India, the Gobi Desert of Mongolia and northern China, and the great deserts in southwestern United States and Mexico. Within the zone to the south of the equator lie south Africa's Kalahari Desert, the deserts of South America, and the vast deserts of Australia.

Humans at Fault? ○ And what of factors other than climatic changes? There is a widespread belief that humans may have contributed to the Sahara's transformation. They may have done so by overgrazing their livestock, continually plowing their fields, felling trees, and cutting down shrubs for fuel. All these activities can expose and loosen the soil and thus leave it especially vulnerable to being blown away by the harsh winds that accompany drought. In time, a vast area can be rendered dusty and barren.

Deserts and desertlike regions may be inhospitable to human life, but they served as the locales for at least two of the world's great early civilizations: the Egyptians and the Sumerians. Both cultures, however, shared a benefit that made their development possible. They flowered in lands blessed with rivers which carried in from distant rain-fed areas the water vital to plant, animal, and human life. The Egyptians built their civilization alongside the Nile River. The Sumerians established themselves between the Tigris and Euphrates rivers in what is today Iraq.

North America

Studies of the rings in pine and juniper trees have shown that about 2,000 years ago a catastrophic drought occurred in what is now the southwestern area of the United States.[4] Lasting twenty-three years, it brought such famine to the Pueblo Indian tribes that they were forced to uproot themselves from the land on which they had lived for centuries and start life anew elsewhere.

Centuries later, in the years just before the outbreak of the American Revolution, drought struck the New England colonists on a number of occasions. Eastern Massachusetts suffered an especially severe attack in 1762. The region's crops were so badly damaged that farmers had to slaughter their livestock because not enough fodder could be stored to feed the animals during the coming winter.

Drought in the West and Midwest ○ When increasing numbers of settlers began venturing into the midwest in the 1800s, they encountered one of the first major droughts on record in the United States. In the spring of 1860 a terrible dryness spread itself over what are now the states of Kansas, Missouri, Iowa, Illinois, Indiana, Minnesota, and Wisconsin.

The heaviest settlement of the American midwest and west came in the years following the Civil War. Thousands of farm and ranch families flooded into the vast region that spread westward from the Mississippi River to the Rocky Mountains, from Texas on the south to the Canadian border on the north. They planted their crops and turned their cattle loose to graze. At first they thought they had ventured into a new Garden of Eden. There was ample rain to nourish their crops and grow the fine rangeland grasses on which their livestock grazed. The weather was so congenial and the rain so plentiful that the railroads, eager for the business of transporting settlers to new homes, used the following advertising slogan to help entice farmers westward: "Rainfall follows the plow." But they soon learned that drought was to invade their Eden at almost regular intervals, sometimes striking with a light touch, sometimes attacking so harshly that it drove hundreds to give up their land and flee back to their old homes in the east.

The most severe of the droughts arrived (and continue to arrive) in the western and midwestern United States on the twenty- to twenty-two-year schedule that scientists suspect is associated with the double sunspot cycle. Droughts thought to have been triggered by the cycle did extensive damage to crops and livestock in the late 1880s, the early 1900s (1910–13), the 1930s, the 1950s, and the 1970s. If indeed the double sunspot cycle is behind the droughts in the west and midwest, it can be expected to bring fresh trouble in the early- to mid-1990s.

What is widely thought to have been the most disastrous American drought of this century was associated with the sunspot cycle. It lay siege to the country for most of the 1930s and did a great deal of economic and social damage. A closer look at this drought will be taken in the next chapter.

Other Major U.S. Droughts ○ The double sunspot cycle, of course, is not associated with all American droughts. In the 1960s and 1980s, for instance, there were severe droughts caused by other factors. The drought of the 1960s, which lasted from 1962 to 1967, struck the northeastern section of the nation and resulted in crop losses and major water shortages all along the Atlantic seaboard from Massachusetts and

Rhode Island in the north to parts of Delaware, Maryland, and West Virginia in the south; it also moved inland to Pennsylvania. It ranks as the longest and most severe drought in the history of the U.S. northeast; many people there contend that its economic harms equaled or surpassed those of the 1930s disaster. The drought of the 1980s struck throughout the entire nation.

Blamed in part for the 1960s drought was the failure of cold air from Canada to move far enough south into the United States to meet warm, moist air coming up from the Gulf of Mexico and cause it to condense and drop rain on the northeastern states. The 1980s drought is strongly suspected of having resulted from the actions of the cold water band, La Niña, thousands of miles to the south in the Pacific Ocean.

To complete the picture of drought's unending attacks, we now turn back to the 1930s—a decade that, because of drought and the violent dust storms it generated, is remembered as "The Dirty Thirties."

CHAPTER SIX

―――○―――

THE DIRTY
THIRTIES

The drought that gave the United States the "Dirty Thirties" began when dry weather struck the Great Plains in 1930.[1] There was rain in 1931, but the dryness returned in 1932 and continued at full strength for at least four years. Between 1936 and 1938, welcome rains managed to sap its fury in some areas. But in others, among them sections of Oklahoma and Kansas, drought stubbornly hung on until the rains of 1941.

Hit by the terrible dryness was the vast expanse of rich grain-growing and ranching land that Americans had long called "the nation's bread basket." It stretched from the Rocky Mountains east to the Mississippi River and beyond, and from the Canadian border south to the Mexican border and the Gulf of Mexico. Hardest hit by the attack were portions of ten states: Montana, Wyoming, North Dakota, South Dakota, Nebraska, Colorado, Kansas, Oklahoma, New Mexico, and Texas.

These ten states were not the only ones harmed. The dryness spread out to affect to some degree virtually the entire nation. In fact, between 1930 and 1936, only two states in the far northeast escaped its wrath—Vermont and Maine.

A Great Calamity

Everywhere on the Great Plains there was disaster. Farmers saw countless plantings of wheat, corn, and other grains wither and die as the intense heat baked the ground dry and left it hard and cracked. In one five-state area—known as the Dust Bowl because of the vicious dust storms that plagued it—the annual

THE 1930s DUST BOWL

wheat and corn crop plunged a frightening 50 to 75 percent. Ranchers watched their cattle die or waste away to gaunt skeletons when the earth became so parched that it could no longer provide the animals with crops for fodder or grass for grazing. Farmers and ranchers alike were left with little or nothing to sell.

For most of these farmers and ranchers, this meant economic ruin. With hardly any income, they still had to buy seed, livestock, and feed if they hoped to remain in business. Consequently, they were forced to use their savings or obtain bank loans—usually putting up their land as collateral—to make the necessary purchases. Each year they planted their new seeds and fed their livestock and hoped that rain would come and put an end to their misery. But each year brought only dryness to kill the fresh plantings and decimate their herds. (It should be noted that there *was* some rain and snow during the years of the drought. But in general, the precipitation measured less than 60 percent of normal—more than enough of a decrease to cause damage of the severest sort.) Soon, their savings were gone and they were too deeply in debt to qualify for new loans. They lost their land to bank foreclosures because they could not meet the payments due on their existing loans. By the mid-1930s, farm families all across the Great Plains were homeless and without a way of making a living.

The federal government tried to alleviate the hardship and save the area's agricultural system by making low-interest loans available and allowing farmers and ranchers to purchase seed and fodder at low prices. But these measures were of scant help in the face of the mounting tragedy.

The Great Flight

It was a tragedy that eventually resulted in one of the greatest mass population shifts the United States has ever seen. Facing starvation and ruin, thousands of families fled the land that they had tilled for years—in many cases, for generations—and went in search of a living elsewhere. Most traveled in old cars, trucks, and even horse-drawn buggies. Some walked, carrying a few precious possessions on their backs. Some—especially those who traveled alone—sneaked aboard freight trains bound in all directions. Many chose as their destination the farmlands of California, which had escaped much of the drought. By the late 1930s, many of the Plains states had lost a major share of their populations.

On arriving at their destinations, the newcomers so glutted the farm labor market that only a few could find work or even a place to live. Thousands of the new arrivals in California* spent their first months sleeping in their cars or rolled up in blankets along the roadsides. Many made their way to the "tent cities" that sprang up in various agricultural areas. Most took any work they could find, doing anything from odd jobs to laboring as fruit pickers and field hands for a few dollars a month.

---

* California was a principal destination for the several hundred thousand people who fled Oklahoma. On arrival, they became known as "Okies," a nickname they found demeaning and insulting. In the 1970s, when a severe drought hit California, several political leaders in Oklahoma said that Californians were welcome to start new lives in Oklahoma and promised (with an understandable note of sarcasm in their voices) that they would not be called "Callies."

The struggle of the uprooted Plains people to begin life afresh in new areas has long stood as a magnificent testament to human strength and endurance. After arriving in their wheezing trucks, with little or no money in their pockets and with scant hopes for the future, many built successful lives for themselves and never again returned to their old homes. Many others did return home at the end of the drought and, just as successfully, started life over again.*

Though the farmers and ranchers were hardest hit by the drought, it soon became the concern of all Americans. With crop and livestock production down, the price of food shot up in grocery stores from one end of the country to the other. The rise came at a time when it could be least afforded. The nation was not only caught in the grip of a terrible drought but was also trapped in the era's Great Depression. Millions of people were out of work. Jobs were almost impossible to find—a fact that made life all the harder for the families that left the Great Plains in the hope of making a living elsewhere. Few people, if any, could afford the increased price of food.

Nature soon made matters worse. First, between 1934 and 1938 grasshoppers swarmed over the Plains states and destroyed more than $315 million in

---

* The mass flight from the stricken Plains states and the hardships endured by the travelers are eloquently described in what is considered to be one of the finest books in American literature, John Steinbeck's *The Grapes of Wrath*. Another excellent book—this one an account of the day-to-day struggle to work the land at home and survive the drought years—is *Empire of Dust*, by Lawrence Svobida, a Kansas farmer.

During the 1930s, barren lands and fear
of starvation triggered the exodus of
thousands of farmers and their families
from the drought-stricken Great Plains.
This photograph, taken by the American
documentary photographer Dorothea Lange,
shows a family traveling with their worldly
possessions on foot to a new home.

crops that were trying desperately to grow. State authorities fought the invaders with poisons, only to have the insects die in heaps on sidewalks and roadways and make the pavement so slippery that pedestrians could not keep their footing and cars slithered out of control. Next, starving rabbits threatened many crops; farmers shot or clubbed them to death, then often ate them because there was no other food available.

Perhaps worst of all, the windstorms that so often accompany droughts began to arrive on the scene in late 1933.[2] They swept across the treeless, stricken land and blew away millions of tons of priceless topsoil.

The Black Blizzards

Quickly nicknamed "black blizzards" and "dusters," these storms ravaged all of the Great Plains region and areas far beyond. One of the first struck in May 1934, when harsh winds roared out of Montana and Wyoming and hurled over 300 million metric tons of topsoil eastward as far as the states of Massachusetts and New York. Some of the dirt was carried out over the Atlantic Ocean and fell on freighters and liners. Portions of Canada also felt the rage of this storm and many of the black blizzards that followed in the next years.

It is easy to see why the storms came to be called black blizzards. Their impending arrival in an area was announced by distant black clouds that, rolling and swirling as they approached, struck many people as looking like "horizontal tornadoes." Actually, the clouds were made up of dirt that was picked up by the winds and sent spinning to altitudes that

*A powerful dust storm looms in
the horizon over the houses of the
Great Plains. Such storms transformed
the landscape into a giant dust bowl.*

often reached 20,000 feet (6,000 m) or more. Sweeping in overhead at speeds clocked at 35 to 60 miles an hour (56 to 96 km per hour), the clouds usually blotted out the sun to the point where visibility was reduced to less than a mile. Lights in offices and homes had to be turned on. So did street lights and automobile headlights. There were times when the clouds obliterated the sun so completely that people could see no more than a few feet in any direction. One woman recalled moments when the darkness was such that she had trouble seeing her hands when she held them up in front of her face.

One type of storm did not qualify as a black blizzard. It brought a brief showery rain that was colored red. This happened when the winds picked up a reddish soil that then mingled with the raindrops to give them their peculiar tint. Though it frightened many of the people caught in it, the red shower proved to be of no health danger to anyone.

On seeing a storm approaching, people ran quickly for shelter indoors. To be caught outside meant having to grope through the darkness with a rag or handkerchief over your face to keep your lungs from filling with the swirling dirt. Many victims were hospitalized with dust-coated and damaged lungs. One young Kansas farmer, caught out in his fields by a storm, died when his lungs filled with dirt. He was not the only victim of the storms; though precise figures have never been compiled, it is estimated that the storms cost at least several hundred lives.

The loss of animal life was much greater. Cattle, for example, quickly choked to death as the dirt flooded into their nostrils and down their throats to their lungs. Thousands of animals are said to have perished in the storms.

A storm could last for hours or days. Throughout the onslaught, dirt piled up in doorways, worked its way through the tiniest openings between windowsills and frames, poured down chimneys, and sometimes covered entire homes and farm buildings. Paint was sandblasted from cars and homes. Mechanical farm gear became clogged and could not be made to operate again until thoroughly cleaned. Businesses and schools were forced to close. At various points, the wind-blown dirt piled in drifts so high on roads and tracks that both vehicular and railroad traffic came to a standstill.

Though all of the Great Plains area suffered from the storms, one region endured the worst storms of all. It was an area of about 50 million acres (20.2 million hectares) that took in portions of five states: Texas, New Mexico, Colorado, Kansas, and Oklahoma. The area, which suffered some forty vicious storms in 1935 alone, became known throughout the nation as the Dust Bowl. The storms and the drought caused the area to lose half its population. Kansas alone lost more than 300,000 of its people by 1939.

Sharing the Blame

The double sunspot cycle may have been behind the drought of the 1930s. But human beings— generations of farmers and ranchers—had to take much of the blame for the loss of millions of tons of rich topsoil in the dust storms.[3]

When the heavy settlement of the Great Plains began after the Civil War, the newly arrived farmers and ranchers found the vast region covered with tough rangeland grasses. The farmers plowed up the land to make way for their plantings, and the ranchers set their cattle loose to graze. As a result, the tough native grasses, which had long served to anchor the topsoil in place, were destroyed. Further, because little or nothing was known of soil conservation at the time, no one bothered to replace them. As a result, with the anchoring grasses gone, the topsoil was gradually loosened and left exposed to the elements. The problem was intensified by the fact that the main crop planted in the region was wheat. Its root system was not strong enough to help hold the loosened soil in place.

As mentioned in Chapter Five, the newcomers soon learned that the Plains region was subject to periodic droughts. Some of the droughts were so severe that they drove many of the settlers back to their homes in the east; left behind were abandoned farms and lost fortunes. All the droughts, especially the one that ran from 1910 to 1913, showed the farmers and ranchers just how quickly the dryness and the dust storms that came hand in hand with it could devastate their lands. But these were lessons that were quickly forgotten when the subsequent years invariably brought plentiful rain. The native grasses continued to be destroyed, with no steps taken to replace them.

The greatest harm occurred during the years following 1914. Until then, much of the Plains region had been devoted to cattle grazing, which did less soil damage than farming. (Grazing animals did not completely destroy the grasses as did the farmer's plow when it turned the ground over.) But a number of factors—among them the growth of the United States and the need of a ravaged Europe for food during and after World War I—caused farming to increase on the Plains from 1914 onward. More and more, the farmer and his plow took over from the rancher. More and more ground was turned over and left exposed to the elements. The increased farming turned the Great Plains into the nation's "bread basket," but it also set the stage for disaster. That disaster came with the winds of the 1930s.

Though the early Plains settlers failed to learn the lessons taught by the region's periodic droughts, the same cannot be said of the people who lived through the "Dirty Thirties." Even while the awful dryness continued to rage unabated, they began working to make certain that they and their lands were never again harmed to the same degree. They instituted a number of safeguards and modern farming practices that, in time, not only blunted future attacks of drought but turned the Great Plains into a richer "bread basket" for the nation than ever before. Despite droughts in the 1950s and 1980s, the region's crop productivity has increased between 200 and 300 percent since the 1930s.

Just what were these safeguards and modern farming practices? The next chapter tells the story of how humans have struggled against the ravages of drought since the beginning of time.

CHAPTER SEVEN

———○———

FIGHTING BACK

The drought of the 1930s was little more than two years old when the first steps were taken to develop prudent agricultural practices that would help safeguard the Great Plains against a similar disaster in the future. The effort was a massive one in which not only the Plains farmers but also scientists, conservationists, local and state governments, and the federal government played a part. Their accomplishments in the next years were many. Here is a sampling of what they did:[1]

○ In 1935, the federal government established the Soil Conservation Service. Its personnel were assigned the task of educating farmers in planting and plowing methods that would help protect the soil from being dried out and would thus assist in keeping it in place when future droughts and their windstorms struck.

○ The United States government sought to protect areas of the Plains by enacting laws calling for federally owned lands to be planted with the range grasses that had once so effectively shielded the topsoil.

○ Local and state governments, with the assistance of the federal government, developed a network of dams for storing water, and a system of canals for carrying it from the facilities to irrigate farmlands for miles around in both good and bad times.

○ Over the years, scientists developed new strains of wheat and corn that needed less water to survive. The new strains also offered the economic advantage of producing crops faster and in greater abundance.

○ Rows of trees were planted throughout the Plains region. The raging wind had been able to sweep tons of soil away because there were so few trees on the prairies to interrupt its flow. The newly planted trees were to serve as windbreaks. By reducing the force of the wind, they not only prevented vast amounts of soil from being carried off but also—because wind speed accelerates evaporation—helped the ground to retain its moisture content. In all, an amazing 185,000 miles (296,000 km) of trees were planted.*

---

* The planting of trees to serve as windbreaks and to beautify the Great Plains was urged by a number of agriculturists as far back as the late 1800s, but the idea was ignored. One of the advocates was Julius Sterling Morton, a Nebraska farmer who later served as a United States Congressman and as U.S. Secretary of Agriculture.

Out of the effort to protect the Great Plains came farming strategies that were put to use in other areas of the nation and so helped the entire country to reduce the effects of future droughts.* For example, farmers began to devote parts of their land to the planting of what are called cover crops; these are crops that not only help to hold the soil in place but also enrich it. Another strategy, known as rotation planting or farming, called for leaving some acreage unplanted one year and planting it the next; the fields that had been planted the preceding year were then allowed to lie idle for a year. Since the idle fields were without roots to take up the water in the ground, the moisture that naturally collected could build up over the course of the year so that it would be in greater supply when the time for the next planting came.

One of the best strategies proved to be contour plowing. In this type of plowing, furrows are made horizontally along slopes rather than up and down them. It provides two principal benefits. The cuts help to hold the soil in place and they enable it to retain more of its moisture. Up- and down-slope cuts allow much topsoil and moisture to slip away from the furrows through the force of gravity.

Actually, there was nothing new about contour plowing. It had been known and practiced since the earliest times by peoples living in mountainous

* Unfortunately, when ample rains came in the 1940s, many Plains farmers forgot about these improved farming methods. They went back to their old ways, plowing up the land to the extent that, when drought and its windstorms returned in the 1950s, the region again faced widespread damage.

Arsenals against drought: (Above) At summertime, an irrigation canal replenishes Idaho's Snake River Plain with water. (Opposite) A farm in Green County, Wisconsin, uses the contour plowing method.

areas, such as those found in parts of China, India, and Peru. There, the farmers had long planted their crops on terraces, which are narrow bands of flattened earth cut into hillsides.[2]

The same holds true for rotation farming (practiced by the ancient Romans and others),[3] tree windbreaks, and many of the facilities developed for irrigation. In all, the efforts to safeguard the Plains were nothing more than the latest steps taken in the war that humans have waged against drought since the dawn of time.

The Ancient War

The early history of the war against drought reveals the inventive skills of our ancient forbears, many of whom lived in the most primitive of cultures. It also demonstrates the universality of human thinking. Many—if not most—ancient societies had little or no contact with each other and knew little or nothing of what distant peoples were doing. Yet, no matter how widely separated they were, they all devised identical methods for handling their water supply and conserving it for use in times of need. They all developed such safeguards as:[4]

> Cisterns, which are large tanks or pools that collect rain water and hold it in storage until needed.

> Dams, likewise used to store water—but in greater amounts than cisterns are able to hold—against times of emergency. The water held in place by a dam is known as a reservoir. It is collected from rivers, streams, and the flow of melting snow from mountainous regions.

Aqueducts, which are channels or canals that carry water from dams, cisterns, mountain streams, and other collection points to farmlands. They are also used for the general distribution of water to towns and cities. The remains of the most unusual of the early aqueducts can still be seen today in Italy; built by the ancient Romans, it is an overhead waterway mounted atop a high structure of stone arches that carries water down from the mountains to the lowlands. The ancient Babylonians and Egyptians constructed wide-ranging systems of underground aqueducts.

What truly stands as a testament to the inventive skills of the ancients is the fact that all their ideas are still used today. The dams used for irrigation purposes in all corners of the world perhaps number in the hundreds of thousands, and the aqueducts that flow away from them to thirsty farm fields undoubtedly cover miles beyond count. The dams, of varying size and constructed of earth and rock or concrete, are widely used in all countries vulnerable to drought, chief among them Australia, China, Egypt, India, the Soviet Union, and the United States.

Of all the dams found across the world, two of the most famous are the Aswan High Dam on Egypt's Nile River and Hoover Dam on the Colorado River.* The Egyptian dam, which was begun in the

---

* In common with many dams, Aswan and Hoover do far more than store water for irrigation purposes. They also generate electricity and, by blocking off rising waters during heavy storms, control floods. Hoover Dam, for example, supplies electricity to Arizona, Nevada, and southern California.

1960s and completed in 1970, stems the flow of the Nile during the rainy season and then releases the water to more than 1 million acres (400,000 hectares) of the nation's farmlands during the dry season. The reservoir that contains the water held in place by the dam is called Lake Nasser (named in honor of the late Gamal Abdel Nasser, for many years the president of Egypt) and stretches for some 300 miles (480 km) along the course of the Nile.

Hoover Dam distributes the Colorado River's water to a vast area. Its construction was begun in 1931, and it was opened in 1936 as Boulder Dam. It was later renamed in honor of President Herbert Hoover. The dam measures 1,242 feet (373 m) in length and stands 726 feet (218 m) high. The reservoir that its construction created is Lake Mead.

Other major dams in the world include: Pati in Argentina; Gardiner in Canada; Dantiwada Left Embankment in India; Afsluitdijk in the Netherlands; San Rogue in the Philippines; Rogun and Nurek in the Soviet Union; and, in the United States, Oroville (California) and Grand Coulee (Washington).

As for aqueducts, two of the most important in the United States are to be found in the nation's west. Both are wide concrete channels that carry water

The Hoover Dam, one of the world's engineering marvels, supplies water and electricity to several states in the Southwest.

great distances to desert regions that have been transformed into rich growing lands over the years by the two facilities. The first transports Colorado River water from Hoover Dam for more than 1,400 miles (2240 km) and, along the way, delivers it to farms in Arizona, Nevada, California, and the northern area of Mexico.

The other, built early in this century, travels for some 250 miles (400 km) from the Sierra Nevada mountains in northern California to the once-parched lands in the southern part of the state.

While all these age-old developments are still in use today, the same cannot be said for other ideas that have come down to us from ancient times.

Strange Ideas

One of the most fascinating aspects of the early war against drought concerns the efforts of humans to induce rain in times of dryness. The ancients, with little or no scientific knowledge, devised ceremonies, based on superstitions and religious beliefs, in the hope of bringing rain to their areas. Such ceremonies were found in all the world's lands where drought struck.[5]

For example, a number of early societies looked on frogs as rain gods; people would beat the little animals during a drought to bully them into bringing rain. In Africa, the Zulus buried children up to their necks in the ground. The aim was to have the gods take pity on the children and allow the rain to fall. In a rain-making ritual in Australia, a primitive tribe covered their people with the blood of medicine men and then coated them with bird down to make them look like clouds. A simpler ceremony was used in the Moluccas, the islands that comprise the Malay archipelago: tribesmen sat together and shook drops of water from sticks while quietly chanting prayers. Here in the United States, the Hopi Indians of Arizona performed dances with snakes to promote rain.

The ancients were not the only ones to use superstitious rituals in the quest for rain. The Europeans of medieval times also had an assortment of practices for putting drought to flight. One called for inducing rain by burning ferns and other plants. In another, statues of saints were dipped in water to punish the saints for allowing a drought to continue after so many people had offered up prayers for its end. This practice was a variation of the ancient ritual of beating the little "frog gods" in retaliation for drought.

To end a drought in France, the people threw flour into a stream and then stirred it with a tree branch. The mixture was supposed to cause a mist to rise from the stream and become a raincloud. A special branch—one from a hazel tree—had to be used for the ceremony.

All these ceremonies and practices strike us today as strange. But they were no stranger than some of the ideas that evolved on the American Great Plains in the late 1800s. There, it was thought that the building of the railroads and the stringing of telegraph lines would help alleviate the periodic droughts for which the region was becoming famous. The belief was that the electricity in the telegraph wires would disturb the atmosphere in a way that would create rain. It was also believed that electricity would be generated in the railroad tracks as trains passed along them and would similarly disturb the atmosphere.

Though we cannot help but be impressed by the human imagination that, from the earliest of times, gave rise to these various ideas and rituals, most of these practices have been dismissed as groundless by moderns. There is, however, one rainmaking idea of old that remains with us today. It has to do with gunpowder.

The idea itself has not been proven, but it remains with us because it played a role in the development of one of the most interesting weapons now used in fighting back against drought—the science of "weather modification."

CHAPTER EIGHT

―――○―――

FIGHTING BACK WITH WEATHER MODIFICATION

Weather modification is the technology that seeks to alter the weather deliberately.[1] Often simply called rainmaking, much of the work of weather modification is centered on methods that will bring the rain and snow needed to end drought, but it also concentrates on ways to disperse the fogs that hamper traffic at the world's airports, to weaken the hailstorms that can do so much damage to crops, and to reduce the awful violence of hurricanes. It attempts to do these works with chemicals.

Weather Modification and Gunpowder

As a science, weather modification began in this century. But its roots can be traced back to the first uses of gunpowder. In the centuries that followed gunpowder's introduction into warfare, a folklore developed around the noise and smoke it created. Many people began to say that cloudbursts often occurred after battles in which cannon and firearms had filled the air with their deafening racket and dense smoke. Later on, the folklore grew when many Americans claimed to have noticed that the fireworks displays at Fourth of July celebrations were often followed by rains and thunder. For years, scientific opinion was split over the matter. Some scientists held that any connection between gunpowder and rain was simply coincidental. Others felt that the noise and smoke did something mysterious to the atmosphere that caused clouds to form and then release their moisture.

Over the years, a number of experiments were attempted to see if cannon fire could, indeed, produce rain.[2] One of the most famous was financed by the U.S. Congress and took place near San Antonio, Texas, in 1892, a year of severe drought there. At noon of a November day, the Army's General R. G. Dyrenforth sent a huge balloon aloft. It was filled with oxygen and hydrogen and fitted with a slow-burning fuse that would cause it to explode two and a half minutes after its release. As the balloon floated into a cloudless sky, two groups of soldiers stood at the ready on hilltops on either side of the General's position. The first manned a battery of eight cannon and one howitzer. The men in the second group were flying kites to which dynamite charges were attached. Electrical wires ran down to the men from the kites.

The balloon made its way to a height of about 4,000 feet (1219 meters) and then blew apart with a roar that was heard (and its concussion felt) for two miles all around. Instantly, the battery of eight guns opened fire. Electrical impulses were sent up the wires to the kites, and dynamite blasts were now added to the din. The eight guns continued to fire at forty-five-minute intervals for the next fifteen hours. New kites were released and blown to bits. All the while, General Dyrenforth and his troops gazed into the smoke-filled sky hoping to see clouds gather.

Finally, at three o'clock the next morning, some rain began to spatter the ground, coming from a few ragged clouds that had started to gather an hour earlier. Dyrenforth ordered another salvo from his eight-gun battery. Then, smiling broadly, he called the experiment off for the night. He was certain that his experiment had produced rain.

But the next days brought disappointment. Dyrenforth continued to send his balloons aloft, fire his cannon, and explode one kite after another. His every effort failed, even when he dispatched larger balloons skyward and added two more guns to his battery.

Despite Dyrenforth's failure, others tried their hand at the same experiment. In 1911, a Texas railroad company set out to end a drought by setting off explosives all day long near the town of Thurber. A little rain fell; no one knew whether it fell by coincidence or was induced by the noise and smoke, but everyone could say one thing for certain—not enough came down to do any good. That same year—and again in 1912—C. W. Post, a well-known manufacturer of breakfast foods, attempted to bring rain to his Texas wheat fields with a series of test firings; he met with no success.

The experiments, especially the one attempted by General Dyrenforth, were widely reported in the press and caused debate all across the country. Some people said that more work should be tried with explosives because, at the least, two of the experiments had been partial successes—*some* rain had fallen. Others condemned the attempts as a waste of time and money. Aside from a useless spattering of rain, all the tests had done nothing but make a deafening racket and foul the air with black smoke. By the turn of the century, scientists and the public were generally agreed that the noise and smoke of explosives didn't have what it took to produce rainclouds.

The answer had to lie somewhere else. It eventually proved to involve the use of chemicals.

Modern Rainmaking

Even after they were discredited, noise and smoke continued to play a part in efforts to produce rain. Now, however, they were used not by scientists, but by men who traveled through the U.S. farmlands and called themselves "rainmakers." Most were charlatans who preyed on the desperation of farmers whenever there was a drought or dry spell. Arriving in wagons and trucks filled with "scientific" equipment, they promised to bring rain quickly—for a fee, of course. They were familiar figures on the American farm scene from the late 1800s through the early decades of this century.

Their "scientific" bag of tricks was a muddle of items. There were horns, bells, wooden clappers, whistles, small cannons, explosive charges, and firearms. Some wagons sported wind machines meant to whip up the air so that, somehow, rain would be coaxed into coming. Others carried stoves or cans of fuel for starting bonfires; the idea was to heat the surrounding air and cause it to rise so that it would condense and become a raincloud.* Some rain-makers brought along "secret formulas"—strange chemical concoctions that they said would miraculously trigger rain when released into the atmosphere. The rainmakers were among the first to employ chemicals in attempts to modify the weather, but their concoctions were useless, devised solely for the purpose of impressing gullible farmers.

The scientific work that finally resulted in the effective use of chemicals for rainmaking and gave us the science of weather modification was achieved in this century.[3] It began in 1911 with the studies by German scientist Alfred Wegener into the behavior of ice crystals and water droplets when they exist together in a cloud. The work was expanded in the 1930s by Scandinavian meteorologist Tor Bergeson. Both men reported that when ice crystals and water droplets are in clouds of sub-freezing temperatures, the crystals grow as the droplets evaporate. The vapor that results from the evaporation gathers and freezes on the crystals and causes them to balloon in size.

This finding led to two practical developments in the 1940s. Dr. Vincent Schaefer, a scientist working for General Electric Laboratories in Schenectady, New York, found that ice crystals could be formed in

---

* The idea that heat generated by bonfires can create atmospheric conditions capable of inducing rain is grounded in scientific fact. But there is a problem in its use. Before the fires can emit sufficient heat to bring rain, they have to be lighted over such an extensive area as to make the whole approach impracticable. Also, the atmosphere must be very moist and unstable before the fires will do any good. These problems were discovered by the American meteorologist James Pollard Espy early in the nineteenth century, during a series of experiments that he conducted in Florida.

a cloud by inserting small amounts of dry ice (solid carbon dioxide) into it; the crystals took shape because dry ice, with a temperature of about $-108°F$ ($-77.8°C$) is able to drop the temperature in a cloud to a freezing $-40°F$ ($-40°C$). Schaefer's fellow worker, Dr. Bernard Vonnegut, then discovered that a smoke composed of tiny silver iodide crystals can produce ice crystals in great quantities at higher temperatures—from about $23°F$ ($-5°C$) downward.

Why were these developments of practical value? Ice crystals that are formed naturally in a low-temperature cloud are able, of course, to fall earthward when they grow heavy enough to overcome gravity and the wind currents holding them aloft. The introduction of solid carbon dioxide or silver iodide crystals causes the temperature in a warmish cloud to plunge to the point where there can be an artificial duplication of the natural process by which the crystals grow when the water droplets evaporate. In all, the chemicals turn the cloud into snow. When the crystals are finally heavy enough to begin falling as snow, they melt on passing through warm air at lower altitudes and arrive on earth as raindrops.

At long last, after centuries of trying to induce rain with anything from beating frogs to artillery barrages, humans had found a way to create it.

Cloud Seeding ○ The process became known as cloud seeding, and the Soviet Union quickly put it to use—but not against drought. The enemy, rather, was the hailstorms that so often attacked the Ukraine, the nation's great wheat-growing area. When hailstones pelted the earth, they could destroy a wheat crop in minutes. Hailstones are chunks of ice that form in especially turbulent clouds. The Soviets adopted, and still use, the practice of firing chemically filled artillery shells and rockets into clouds to turn the hailstones into rain.

The strategy works this way. On reaching a certain height, the shells explode and spew their cargoes of dry ice or silver iodide throughout the clouds. The water droplets in the clouds collect on the arriving crystals rather than on the chunks of ice that are forming as hailstones. The result is that the stones are reduced in size or, in some instances, eliminated altogether. The water droplets then fall principally as rain.*

Ever since trying the strategy, Soviet scientists have reported that it has produced successful results. They claim that it has reduced hail damage to grapes and other crops by as much as 60 to 90 percent.

Cloud Seeding: A Real Help? ○ When cloud seeding was first developed, many people thought that it was the weapon that would finally put an end to drought. All that had to be done to bring rain was to release the chemicals from aircraft or send them up from the ground in the heat created by generators. But such has not proved to be the case. While there is no doubt that the process works, it has certain limitations and has triggered a number of questions about its effectiveness.

Its most serious limitation in the fight against drought stems from two basic facts. First, as its very name makes clear, clouds must be present before the technique can be employed. Second, not all clouds

* Long before these firings, the Soviets had been shooting regular artillery shells into the skies above the Ukraine to thwart the hailstorms, acting on the belief that cloudbursts do indeed follow battles.

bear rain; experiments have shown that seeding will not work unless the clouds on the scene are capable of bringing rain. Unfortunately, drought is usually present under cloudless skies or under what are called fair-weather clouds—clouds that, because of their content and the surrounding atmospheric conditions, cannot produce rain. In both these instances, seeding is a helpless tool.

The questions about the effectiveness of seeding have been prompted by various experiments that have produced mixed results. On the one hand, experimental seedings in Israel, Tasmania, and in the mountains of Colorado have triggered an estimated 10 to 30 percent more rain than would have been expected without seeding. But test seedings in other areas have produced scant rain or none at all. For example, while the Colorado seeding upped the rainfall, an experiment above the nearby Great Plains brought little or no rain. In fact, it was felt that there had been a *decrease* in precipitation in sections of the prairies. This caused many farmers, and a number of weather scientists, to wonder if seeding might increase the rainfall in one area at the expense of a neighboring region.

Despite the estimated rainfall increases noted in the Israel, Tasmania, and Colorado experiments, scientists have never been able to resolve the most troublesome question of all: How can we judge beyond doubt that seeding actually increases the amount of rain in an area? The question cannot be answered because there is no way of knowing how much rain would have fallen naturally had seeding not occurred. Would there have been less rain, an equal amount of rain, or more rain?

Another problem: Seeding is an expensive process. In the minds of many scientists, it must increase the rain or snow in a region by at least 10 percent before it can be of significant benefit to agriculture (and to the production of hydroelectric power). At present, on the basis of experiments around the world, many scientists doubt that it is able to do so and wonder if the negligible results are worth the expense.

Scientists pose yet another riddle: Since seeding will not work unless rain-bearing clouds are present, might not there be rain anyway if seeding is not tried? If so, would it be wiser to wait and see if nature takes its course rather than going to the expense of seeding? There are, of course, no answers to the riddle.

Other aspects of seeding have also come into question. The Soviet claims of successful seedings against hailstorms are doubted by scientists in other countries where experiments to duplicate the Soviet seedings have been attempted. The attempts have failed to yield the results claimed by the Soviet scientists.

One use of seeding, however, has proven its value. It is successfully used by a number of countries to disperse the fogs that so often plague and delay the traffic at their airports.

At present, we know how to make rain, but we have as yet to learn just how valuable this tool may prove itself to be in the age-old war against drought. Perhaps the continuing research on seeding will one day show us the answer. Meanwhile, we still must face an ugly fact and take steps to protect ourselves against it: drought—after proving itself an enemy in the past and in the present—now looms as an enemy of the future, perhaps a greater enemy than ever before.

CHAPTER NINE

―――――○―――――

THE FUTURE ENEMY

Many scientists fear that drought will be an especially dangerous enemy in the future because of two recent atmospheric developments. First, there are indications that the earth's climate is entering a period of cooling. Second, there is the increasing heat being generated by what is known as the "greenhouse effect."

These developments—one having to do with coolness and the other with heat—are exact opposites. But many scientists hold that they bring the same result: droughts in increasing number.

A Global Cooling Trend

Throughout its long history, our planet has periodically experienced major changes in its climate.[1] They have all exerted a significant effect on the ability of the hydrologic cycle to manufacture the evapotranspiration and condensation that nourishes the earth with precipitation. There have been times of warmth when water covered many areas that are now dry land or when there was sufficient precipitation to make fertile garden spots of certain regions. There have been times of such great heat that precipitation disappeared and left once-fertile areas as barren deserts.

Conversely, there have been times when the climate cooled so much that great ice ages occurred. These were periods of intense cold when glaciers— massive sheets of ice that can range in thickness measuring up to hundreds or even thousands of feet—covered great sections of the world.

And there have been eras of climatic cooling that, while not cold enough to form widespread glaciers, have affected the actions of the hydrologic cycle and brought such surprises as heavy snow to regions where it had never before fallen. These have been called "little ice ages." One of the best known ran from about 1550 to the mid-1800s, after which there was a warming trend.*

In recent years, climatologists have collected weather data that suggests we are entering a new period of global cooling. The world's climate, after warming since the mid-1800s, began to cool again around 1950 and has continued to cool ever since. Conversely, very recent global studies appear to indicate that there has been a warming trend since the 1970s. And so the worldwide cooling could pass quickly or could persist a long while. Such climatic periods can only be identified over long stretches of time.

---

* Though this "little ice age" did not cause glaciers to form throughout the world, it did result in an expansion of the ice pack that covers the Arctic Ocean. The growth of the pack put a stop to the early Norse voyages across the North Atlantic.

A New "Little Ice Age"? ○ If the cooling period proves to be a long one—as many scientists believe it will—climatologists tell us not to fear that we're in for a time when glaciers will cover much of the world. The last *great* ice age arrived close to two million years ago after the global climate had slowly cooled over a span of several million years. It lasted until some 10,000 years ago and lay its icy mantle over Canada, the northern United States, Russia and northern Europe, parts of South America and Australia, and the entire continent of Antarctica. Rather, the present cooling trend, if prolonged, could lead us to another *little* ice age. En route, we can look forward to unstable weather patterns, somewhat lower year-round temperatures, colder summers with frosty mornings at times, more severe winters—and droughts.

Yes, a cooling climate can bring on droughts just as efficiently as great heat because it, too, is able to create atmospheric conditions that upset the hydrologic cycle and thwart its ability to produce precipitation. Remember that the two coldest locations on earth—the north and south polar regions—are classed as deserts. They receive scant rain and suffer permanent drought because the icy air hampers all phases of the cycle.

The theories on the causes of cooling trends that can lead to little and great ice ages are many. One holds that the sun varies its energy output on occasion and emits less heat than usual during cooling periods. Another argues that the inclination of the earth's axis and the shape of the earth's orbit trigger the problem by changing from time to time. Still another contends that the clouds of dust from volcanic eruptions—and from meteorites hitting the earth—so choke the atmosphere that the amount of solar heat reaching the earth is significantly reduced.

Times of coolness can be either short- or long-lived. For proof of what either length of duration can do, we need look only at two phenomena. First, there were the havocs—including far-flung droughts—wrought by the Pacific Ocean's cold La Niña during its appearance in 1988. Second, there is the fate that befell a number of areas when the last great ice age lay its hand on the world.

It is known that, prior to that time, tropical plants thrived in southern England and the Yukon region of North America. There were tropical and semi-tropical forests inhabited by monkeys and apes in Europe. In the several million years of worsening climate that preceded the arrival of the glaciers, both the tropical vegetation and animals began to migrate southward. The lands where they had once thrived were never the same again.

Some climatologists who believe that we are embarked on a prolonged period of cooling say that it may mark the first step towards another great ice age when glaciers will again cover the world. But there is no reason to call off next Sunday's picnic. On the basis of their studies, they predict that the next great ice age lurks about 10,000 years in the future. What seems to be in store for us—if the belief that the cooling period will be an extended rather than a passing one proves true—is the continuing and growing presence of drought in our lives.

The Greenhouse Effect

The *greenhouse effect* is a term that has come into worldwide use within the past several decades.[2] It refs to a phenomenon that intensifies atmospheric heat. Here is how it works.

The sun is the source of most of the earth's heat. It radiates heat that reaches us principally in the form of visible and invisible (near-ultraviolet) rays. On their arrival, the earth absorbs some of their heat and reradiates the rest back out into space. Much of the reradiated heat, however, never reaches its destination. Rather, its path is blocked by the water vapor and the gases—chief among them carbon dioxide (CO_2)—that make up much of the atmosphere. The gases absorb the heat and then reradiate it back to earth. The outcome is that the earth is heated even more.

In absorbing and then reradiating the heat back to earth, the water vapor and gases are said to be acting much like the glass roof of a garden greenhouse. The glass allows heat to enter the greenhouse and keeps it there by reradiating it downward when it rises and attempts to escape.*

Because of the greenhouse effect, the air temperature at the earth's surface is warmer by about 32°F (17.8°C) than it would otherwise be.

One point about the greenhouse effect that puzzles many people needs to be clarified before we go on. We've mentioned the fact that the dust from volcanic eruptions and meteorite crashes, when blanketing the earth, prevents much of the sun's heat from entering the atmosphere and causes temperatures to cool. Why do not carbon dioxide and the

---

* Technically, it is not completely accurate to compare the atmospheric reflection to the actions of a greenhouse. This is because, in great part, the heating in a greenhouse is due to preventing outside air from entering, mixing with, and cooling the inside air.

other gases in the atmosphere do the same thing? The reason is that, so far as the sun's heat is concerned, they are "transparent." The sun's rays pass directly through them on the trip to the earth's surface. It is only when heat is being reradiated by the earth that it is absorbed by the gases and the water vapor.

Why the Worry About the Greenhouse Effect? ○ The greenhouse effect has been with us ever since the atmosphere and such gases as carbon dioxide came into being and has done no great harm in all that time. Then why are climatologists so worried about it today, with many of them predicting it will bring drought and other weather upheavals in the near future?

The answer is that since the beginning of the Industrial Age more than a century ago, the world's factories have burned increasing amounts of fossil fuels—coal, gas, and oil—belching forth their carbon dioxide content in clouds of smoke. As a result, the newly produced carbon dioxide has strengthened the barrier that prevents reradiated heat from escaping into space. More and more of the heat is reradiated back to earth, thus gradually raising the air temperatures.

At first glance, the temperature increases caused by the growing greenhouse effect seem small. In the late 1890s, a Swedish chemist named Svante Arrhenius became concerned about the great amounts of coal then being burned by industry and calculated that, given a sufficient amount of time, the carbon dioxide being pumped into the atmosphere by the burnings could result in a warming of the globe by 9°F (5°C). Current estimates hold that a doubling of the atmosphere's carbon dioxide content will produce global temperatures three to eight degrees higher than they have been in recent decades. If so, the earth will be warmer than it has been for the past two million years.

According to recent computer studies, this temperature increase will not bring about the same result everywhere. They indicate minor changes in the temperatures in tropical areas, but predict that temperatures in the northern and southern latitudes near the polar regions could rise by 11° to 16°F (6° to 9°C). The computer studies have been unable to gauge what changes may occur in various local areas. In our century, the overall global temperature has risen about 1°F (.56°C).

While a general global increase of 3° to 8°F (1.6° to 4.4°C) may seem small, climatologists warn us that it can produce a number of varied results. Because nature is a thing of complex and delicate balances, even the slightest atmospheric change can prove of great significance. Climates can be dramatically altered over great areas or within confined locales. Probable changes include heavier rains in the tropics, stormier winters in some regions, and hotter, drier summers in others. Additionally, the more dramatic increase in the higher northern and southern latitudes would cause a melting of the polar glaciers and ice packs in summer, with a resultant rise in ocean levels that could be of risk to some coastlines.

Changes such as these can force the people in the affected regions to alter the way they work, spend their leisure time, dress, and build their houses. Animals and plant life can be disrupted. For some areas, the changes may be beneficial, bringing rains that improve the local agriculture. But other areas may well see their agriculture damaged by an increasing number of droughts. There could then be, as in the United States in the 1930s, great migrations of farmers to new regions when they can no longer make a living off the soil at home.

Climatologists predict that if the amount of carbon dioxide in the atmosphere doubles what it was prior to the Industrial Age, the average global precipitation is likely to rise by 7 to 11 percent. But for some areas, increased precipitation also heightens the possibility of drought conditions. This can occur because increased evaporation (caused by a warmer atmosphere) reduces the moisture content available in the soil for growing plants. These very factors can also lead to a reduction in an area's annual precipitation.

Especially vulnerable to these is threats is North America's Great Plains region. Studies of what the greenhouse effect can do in the future indicate that severe droughts—such as those seen in the 1930s, 1950s, and 1980s—will strike there with greater frequency than ever before. If things turn out this way, the food supply of the nation—and the world—will be jeopardized tragically. The United States and Canada are the chief suppliers of grain to other countries in times of drought.

Will the Carbon Dioxide Content Double? ○ What are the chances that the atmosphere's carbon dioxide content will soon double what it was prior to the Industrial Age? If nothing is done to reduce the amounts of CO_2 currently being spewed into the air, the chances are excellent. The global burning of fossil fuels is presently increasing by about 4 percent per year. If the burning continues at its present rate, the concentration of carbon dioxide in the atmosphere will be double the pre-Industrial Age level somewhere around the year 2025.

The increase of carbon dioxide has been accelerated over the years by factors other than industrial emissions. A principal one has been the growing use of the automobile in all its forms—passenger car, truck, bus, and recreational vehicle. Another is the deforestation that has taken place in many areas, among them South America's Amazon Basin. The tropical rain forests there are being cut down for the manufacture of commercial forest products and to clear the land for settlement, agriculture, and development of the region's recently discovered oil resources. It is estimated that as much as a fifth to a quarter of the Amazon rain forest has already been cut down and the pace is accelerating annually.

The danger there—and wherever else deforestation is occurring—is that trees absorb and hold great amounts of CO_2 in their trunks. When they are cut and removed, their great storage capacity is lost. And, when they are burned, their carbon dioxide is released into the atmosphere.

In 1988 alone, humans added an estimated 5.5 billion tons (4.9 billion metric tons) of carbon dioxide to the atmosphere through the burning of fossil fuels. The denuding of the world's forests added another 0.4 billion to 2.5 billion tons (0.36 billion to 2.26 billion metric tons). If the world's use of products that involve carbon dioxide burning in their manufacture or use continues to grow at the present rate of 3 percent a year, we can expect to be disgorging 10 billion tons (9 billion metric tons) of CO_2 into the atmosphere annually by the year 2010.

The Full Impact of the Greenhouse Effect ○
Though warning that the greenhouse menace is annually growing greater, many scientists prophesy that we will not feel its full impact for another forty or more years. This is because the rise in temperature is being currently slowed by two factors—first, the great ability of the world's oceans to cool the atmosphere and, second, the general cooling trend on which the global climate seems embarked.* The scientists predict that the full impact of the greenhouse effect will finally be felt sometime between 2030 and 2050.

Not all climatologists and environmental experts, however, agree with this prediction. There are many who argue that the greenhouse effect is presently overriding the global cooling trend and that we are feeling the effect's first harsh touches. To substantiate their view, they point to weather records showing that five of the warmest years in the past one hundred years all occurred between 1980 and 1988 and were marked by everything from violent monsoon rains to searing heat waves, forest fires, and severe droughts.

But it must be pointed out that the claim of a connection between the weather upheavals in 1988 and the greenhouse effect is presently under serious doubt. There is general agreement among climatologists that the trouble was caused by the Pacific's cold water band, La Niña.

---

* The cooling trend may be already ending. As previously mentioned, recent global studies give indication that there has been a warming trend since the 1970s.

We have never coped with the greenhouse effect before and thus have no past experience on which to predict exactly what it will do in the future. Many of the predictions of what might happen if the effect goes unchecked are based on computer projections. Climatologists look on these projections not as unarguable truths but, to use their term, as "scenarios" of what *might* occur.

At this moment, no one can say whether the various predictions will prove accurate or inaccurate. But we cannot take the chance that they will eventually prove inaccurate. We all must take action to protect the world against the possibility of more droughts and the terrible suffering they can bring.

But what, exactly, can we do?

CHAPTER TEN

―○―

CONQUERING
THE FUTURE ENEMY

If we wish to help defeat the future enemy, there are three steps each of us can take, no matter our age, our position in life, or where we live. Indeed, they are steps that we *must* take because many of the forces that are threatening us with more frequent droughts in the future are also threatening to destroy the total environment of the world.

Work to Save the Atmosphere

To safeguard against not only the droughts that the greenhouse effect may bring but also the awful possibility that pollution in general will render the atmosphere too "unbreathable" to sustain life, we must tirelessly urge governments, industries, and all people to join in the current struggle to end the problem of air pollution or at least bring it under control.

The greenhouse effect is but one menace posed by the worldwide atmospheric contamination that has been the most terrible gift bequeathed to us by the Industrial Age. Air pollution is choking our major cities, heightening the risk of respiratory and other diseases, damaging the quality of life for millions of people, and ripping a hole in the ozone layer, the high-altitude shield that, formed by the action of ultraviolet radiation on oxygen, protects us from harm by the sun's rays.

Various countries, the United States among them, are now individually pursuing programs intended to reduce the dangerous emissions caused by the burning of fossil fuels in factories and automobile engines.[1] Likewise, various governments, again individually, have mounted programs aimed at outlawing certain methods by which the chlorofluorocarbons (CFCs), which have proven to be a particular danger to the ozone layer, are released into the atmosphere. The United States is a leader in the movement against the chlorofluorocarbons, having banned their use in spray cans more than a decade ago, in 1978.

In the mid-1970s the U.S. Congress enacted the Clean Air Act, which is dedicated to reducing the nation's atmospheric pollution. Unfortunately, the Act has not been as strenuously enforced everywhere as many people had hoped. At present, some sixty-two American cities are failing to meet the carbon dioxide and ozone standards set forth in the Act.

We need to cooperate in all such programs and measures designed to fight pollution (even if some cause us discomfort and the loss of some modern conveniences) and insist that they be constantly obeyed, enforced, and strengthened. And we especially need to encourage the ongoing search to devise and develop fuels—especially non-petroleum automotive products—that can serve as alternatives to the fossil fuels. In 1988, the U.S. Congress passed a bill encouraging automobile manufacturers to develop cars capable of operating on non-petroleum fuels or fuels in which gasoline ·is blended with alcohols.

International Actions ○ Support must also go to an international movement now under way against the growing greenhouse effect and pollution in general. Two worldwide groups—the World Meteorological Organization and the International Council of Scientific Unions—are presently working to coordinate worldwide research into the problem. The Canadian government in 1987 sponsored a meeting of environmental leaders from a number of countries; the conference called for carbon dioxide emissions to be reduced by 20 percent by the year 2005. In 1988, many ambassadors and ministers to the United Nations pointed out the need for the world's leaders to address the problem of the greenhouse effect and take action to solve it.

In 1986, eight years after the United States had banned the spray-can use of chlorofluorocarbons, an international conference at Montreal, Canada, took a major step against CFCs. The several nations in attendance entered an agreement known as the Montreal Protocol. It froze CFC production at its 1986 levels and called for a 50 percent cut in CFC production and usage by 1998. Since 1986, thirty-five nations have signed the pact. These reductions, however, are widely viewed as inadequate safeguards against the CFC dangers. The wording of the

Protocol leaves the door open for future discussions leading to additional cuts.

Such action may lead to an international treaty for the protection of the atmosphere. Several nations—among them Canada, Norway, and the Netherlands—are dedicated to international negotiations that may result in such an agreement.

End Thoughtless Deforestation ○ We need, too, to add our voices to the growing worldwide call for an end to the thoughtlessness seen in many deforestation programs. Concerned people everywhere are urging that needless over-cutting be halted, and are demanding that all felled trees be replaced with new trees that will restore the beauty of the denuded regions and help to absorb dangerous carbon dioxide. Obviously, if we are to have homes and other of life's necessities, a certain amount of cutting is necessary. But it must be a reasonable amount. Over-cutting and the additional burning that it entails are not simply adding CO_2 to the atmosphere. They are also worsening the upset in the balance of nature that comes with any deforestation and are accelerating the extinction of much plant and animal life.

However, the battle to provide enough new trees to offset the amounts of CO_2 being spewed into the atmosphere promises to be an uphill one. Recent estimates hold that 360 million acres (144 million hectares) of forests being newly planted will provide enough trees to absorb up to 780 million tons (707 million metric tons) of carbon dioxide annually. This absorption would be enough to counter about one-eighth of the billions of tons of CO_2 being released worldwide by the present burning of fossil fuels.

Work for Better Methods of Water Preservation ○
Early in this book, we said that water is not lost when the hydrologic cycle circulates it into the atmosphere and then returns it to earth as precipitation. However, despite this fact, precious water *is* being lost to us today in a certain way.

The industrial, public, and individual actions that are polluting the atmosphere are also polluting our fresh water supply, and our ocean water as well. We are blindly dumping everything from toxic industrial wastes to public garbage and individual litter into our rivers and streams. We are also allowing toxic wastes to seep into the water supply beneath the earth's surface by burying them, often in containers that are not completely leak-proof. While the water that is being damaged is not actually lost to the world, much of it has been rendered so filthy and poisonous that its *use* has been lost.

Poisoned water is already killing plants, fish, and animals. We are warned against bathing in or drinking the water in certain areas lest our own health be threatened. In fact, there is in Peru a river so contaminated with poisonous industrial waste that fish are said to be unable to survive in it more than ten seconds.

The loss of fresh water to such poisoning is bound to increase with the passing years—with the water perhaps remaining lost to us for generations or even for all time to come—unless we give the strongest support to current and future programs aimed at putting an end to its polluting.[2] Today's efforts are seeking anti-pollution measures that include the efficient and safe storage of dangerous industrial wastes; techniques for removing toxins from industrial wastes before the wastes are released into a river or ocean; improved methods of refuse disposal; and the consumer use of biodegradable products that, by their nature, will not add to the world's rising heaps of garbage.

In addition to the efforts aimed at preserving our fresh water supply by cleansing it of pollutants, steps have been taken in recent years to reduce its rates of evaporation and seepage so that it is always available to us in greater amounts. For example, to thwart evaporation, more and more underground pipelines are being constructed so that water can be kept safely away from the sun's heat when being transported from place to place. To prevent loss through seepage into the earth, an increasing number of irrigation canals are being lined with concrete. Such construction projects should be applauded and encouraged.

Increasing the Water Supply ○ Some countries have taken steps to increase their fresh water supply by establishing desalination—or desalting—facilities. These are plants that extract fresh water from ocean water by removing the latter's salt content. The removal is achieved through various processes. They include the use of great heat, high pressure, freezing, and, in some instances, chemicals. Desalination plants are to be found in such nations as Greece, Israel, Italy, Kuwait, Mexico, the Soviet Union, and the United States.

A number of countries tap into stores of water called *aquifers*. The term comes from the Latin words *aqua* (meaning "water") and *ferre* (meaning "to carry"), and refers to groundwater that is locked in porous rocks far beneath the earth's surface. The

This desalination plant contains vats that boil and distill salt out of seawater.

water does not collect in pools but lies within the rocks, soaking and turning them into what many geologists describe as "wet sponges." The water is customarily found in such porous rocks as sandstone, gravel, and sand, and in rocks with splits in them.

Aquifers are proving to be a rich source of previously untapped water in many lands, especially those such as Israel, Egypt, and Morocco which are located in arid regions. But prudence must be exercised in employing the aquifers. If they are not to run dry, their water must not be withdrawn at a faster rate than it is replaced by the surrounding underground water. This problem is currently endangering one of the largest aquifers in the world—the Ogallala Aquifer in the United States. A vast underground reservoir that stretches from South Dakota to Texas, it has been suffering a drop in its level because its water is being expended more quickly than it is being renewed.

Work to Conserve Our Fresh Water Supply o
When living through the droughts of recent years, we have learned many of the steps that can be taken to preserve water.[3] Industries, for example, have been urged—or ordered by local governments and water districts—not to use water indiscriminately in their manufacturing processes but only during limited periods of the day. Towns and cities have had their restaurants stop serving glasses of water at the tables. Some towns and cities have closed their public swimming pools. Some have watered the plants in their parks and alongside their roadways with reclaimed or recycled water, that is, water unfit for human consumption.

Families and individuals have voluntarily practiced a wide variety of water conservation measures during droughts. The measures have included taking fewer showers and baths, refraining from flushing toilets after every use, and placing gravel-filled bottles in toilet tanks to reduce the amount of water expended in flushing.

Families and individuals have also been ordered by their local governments and water districts to follow certain water-saving rules. For example, they have been instructed not to hose down sidewalks, walkways, patios, and driveways. They have been prohibited from washing cars or limited to washing them only with hoses equipped with shut-off nozzles. They have been told to have all leaks in their water pipelines repaired in a matter of hours, usually no more than forty-eight. Failure to follow these rules often results in fines and even imprisonment.

All these conservation measures, whether they have been undertaken voluntarily or at the order of local authorities, have proved of great value during times of drought. But, when the drought has passed, they have been set aside and the public has gone back to its normal use of water. The return to normalcy has been unfortunate because it has seen an untold amount of water wasted through needless use. We would be much wiser to keep many conservation practices in use during times when water is plentiful. This would ensure that we have more water than usual on hand when a drought does strike and that each of us would be better prepared to do what we must do to save water at that time.

Fortunately, they are the simplest of measures, ones that all of us can follow in our daily lives without any hardship whatsoever. They will save countless gallons of water. To see this for yourself, why not try them for a month. Then check your family's next water bill when it arrives and compare it with the previous bill. The bills will specify the amounts of water used during the respective billing periods and clearly show how many gallons you've saved. You'll be surprised at how much water you've been wasting in the past. Here are some of the things you can do:

- ○ If you take showers, check the length of time you usually stand under the water. Let's say that it averages out to ten minutes. Cut that time in half.

- ○ If you prefer baths, measure the depth to which you usually fill the tub. Suppose it comes out to an average of five or six inches. Reduce it to about three inches.

- ○ When brushing your teeth, do not let the tap water run all of the time. Turn it off when actually brushing. Turn it on just long enough to rinse out your mouth.

- ○ Do you use a hose when washing your car? Even if it has a shut-off nozzle, refrain from using it when soaping the car. Use a bucket of soapy water instead. Use the hose only when rinsing down the car. You'll get the car just as clean as usual, but with far less water.

- ○ When watering the plants in your garden, wet them down with a few buckets of water rather than with a hose. This concentrates the flow of water on the plants rather than spraying it over the whole backyard or patio.

By filling a bucket with soapy water instead
of spraying directly from a garden
hose, these two boys are able to conserve
water when washing the family car.

○ When cleaning a sidewalk, patio, or other concrete area, sweep it before washing it down. Countless gallons of water are wasted when you attempt to hose away leaves, gravel, and scattered bits of debris. Save the hose for the final rinsing.

Think of other steps you can take to help conserve water and put them to use along with the above suggestions. With a little thought, you'll undoubtedly come up with some fine ideas. And, please, practice water conservation for extended periods of time and not just for the month that was suggested above. It was suggested as a test period, one that will enable you to check your water bills to see exactly how much good you're doing. If you stick to your practices for an extended period, they'll become habits that can last a lifetime.

Talk to your friends about drought and encourage them to help conserve water. The more people who become involved, the better. Look at it this way: the populations of three countries that have long suffered droughts—Australia, Canada, and the United States—total more than 388 million people. It takes no mathematical skill at all to gauge the staggering amount of water that would be harvested if every Australian, Canadian, and U.S. citizen did no more than save one gallon per day—and this can be done simply by shutting off the bathroom shower one to two seconds earlier than usual. Multiply that total by 365 and you have a monumental saving of more than 136 trillion gallons per year. To propel the totals to even more astronomical heights, get out your pencil or calculator and see the results if each of those 388 million people saved five, ten, or fifteen gallons a day—savings that can be easily realized.

It is vital that as many people as possible become involved in a lifelong personal water conservation program. Fresh water is of absolute necessity to our survival and to the survival of the plants and animals that share the world with us. Our supply of it has always been threatened by drought, and the threat promises to be a growing one in the future. With a menace that can bring intense suffering and world-wide food shortages looming so large on the horizon, it becomes everyone's duty to protect everyone else against drought and the terrible, frightening damage it can do.

SOURCE NOTES

———————o———————

Chapter One
Drought: Portrait of the Enemy

1. The text material on the definitions for drought are developed from: L. J. Battan, *Weather in Your Life* (New York: W. H. Freeman, 1983), 60; T. P. Johnson, *When Nature Runs Wild* (Mankato, Minn.: Creative Education Press, 1968), 76–77; M. Micallef, *Floods & Droughts* (Carthage, Ill.: Good Apple, 1985), 11; B. Tufty, *1001 Questions Answered About Natural Land Disasters* (New York: Dodd, Mead, 1969), 236–37.

2. The text material and footnotes on the insidious manner in which drought strikes are developed from: L. J. Battan, *Harvesting the Clouds: Advances in Weather Modification* (New York: Doubleday, 1969), 7–8; D. B. Fradin, *Disaster! Droughts* (Chicago: Children's Press, 1983), 9, 35–37; T. P. Johnson, 78; T. Loftin, "Drought: Clouds of Dust, Storms of Fire," a chapter in *Powers of Nature* (Washington, D.C.: National Geographic Society, 1978), 132–33, 142; B. Rudolph, "The Drought's Food-Chain Reaction," *Time*, July 11, 1988, 40; Tufty, 237, 241–44.

3. The material on the agricultural and economic losses suffered in the U.S. drought of 1988 is developed from: C. Petit, "Drought Still Grips Plains, Experts Say," *San Francisco Chronicle*, January 16, 1989; "Senate Approves $3.9 Billion in Farm Drought Aid," *San Francisco Chronicle*, August 9, 1988; "House Oks Drought Relief," *San Francisco Chronicle*, August 10, 1988; "Drought Called Costliest U.S.

Natural Disaster," *San Francisco Chronicle* (from a *Los Angeles Times* report), August 13, 1988.

4. The material on the Soviet Union droughts of 1972 and 1975 is developed from: "Soviet Grain Shipments Halted," *Facts on File*, October 12, 1974, 830; "Russians Buy More Canadian Wheat," *Facts on File*, August 2, 1975, 548–49.

5. The material on the droughts that struck Africa's Sahel region in the 1960s, 1970s, and 1980s is developed from: L. R. Brown, Project Director, *State of the World 1989: A Worldwatch Institute Report on Progress Toward a Sustainable Society* (New York: W. W. Norton, 1989), 62; R. A. Bryson and T. J. Murray, *Climates of Hunger: Mankind and the World's Changing Weather* (Madison, Wis.: University of Wisconsin Press, 1977), 96–98; S. H. Schneider and R. Londer, *The Coevolution of Climate and Life* (San Francisco: Sierra Club Books, 1984), 374.

6. The material on the lives lost to drought as compared to those lost to hurricanes, floods, and earthquakes is developed from: Dolan, *The Old Farmer's Almanac Book of Weather Lore* (Dublin, N.H.: Yankee Books, 1988), 182; *The World Almanac and Book of Facts, 1986* (New York: Newspaper Enterprise Association, 1985), 688–89.

7. Battan, *Weather in Your Life*, 60.

8. The material on the British drought of 1976 is developed from: Loftin, 155–56.

9. The material on the damage to the world's grain crops and the decline in global food supplies is developed from: " '88 Drought Feared as a World Catastrophe," *New York Times*, October 2, 1988; L. R. Brown, "Drought Highlights Decline in Global Food Supplies," *San Francisco Chronicle*, August 17, 1988.

Chapter Two
The Nature of the Enemy

1. The text material and footnotes on the hydrologic cycle and the effects of drought on it are developed from: L. J. Battan, *Weather in Your Life*, 12–13, 45–46; R. Hardy, P. Wright, J. Kington, J. Gribbin, *The Weather Book* (Boston: Little, Brown, 1982), 29–30, 51, 62–63; C. L. Mantell and A.M. Mantell, *Our Fragile Water Planet: An Introduction to the Earth Sciences* (New York: Plenum Press, 1976), 41–43, 48; L. D. Rubin, Sr. and J. Duncan, *The Weather Wizard's Cloud Book: How You Can Forecast the Weather Accurately and Easily by Reading the Clouds* (Chapel Hill, N.C.: Algonquin Books of Chapel Hill, 1970),

10–13; T. Sanders, *Weather: A User's Guide to the Atmosphere* (South Bend, Ind.: Icarus Press, 1985), 9, 137, 139, 142–43, 146; A. N. Strahler, *The Earth Sciences* (New York: Harper & Row, 1963), 439–442; J. Weiner, *Planet Earth* (New York: Bantam Books, 1986), 294.

2. The text material and footnotes on the world's supply of surface and ground water and how it is depleted by drought are developed from: Battan, *Weather in Your Life,* 45; P. E. Lehr, R. W. Burnett, H. S. Zim, *Weather* (Racine, Wis.: Western Publishing, 1975), 12, 30, 67, 147; Tufty, 251–52, 266–69; Strahler, 444.

3. The text material and footnotes on the types of drought is developed from: Hardy et al, 142–43; Lehr et al., 67, 147; Tufty, 253–54; Sanders, 136–37, 150.

Chapter Three
Why Drought Strikes

1. The text material and footnotes of how changes in wind force can induce a drought are developed from: Dolan, 76–79; Hardy et al., 92; Lehr et al., 56–59.

2. The text material and footnotes on how a shift in wind direction can induce drought is developed from: Fradin, 30–31; Hardy et al., 32, 91, 95, 134–35; Schneider and Londer, 157–58.

3. The text material and footnotes on atmospheric pressure and its relationship to drought are developed from: Tufty, 239, 254, 256; Lehr et al., 62; Hardy et al., 132.

4. The text material and footnotes on the contributions of land and sea to drought are developed from: Battan, *Weather in Your Life,* 69–70; Dolan, 40–41; Tufty, 255, 271.

Chapter Four
Drought in Cycles

1. The material on the evidence in support of cyclical drought is developed from: B. Tufty, 249; J. Weiner, 99.

2. The text material and footnotes on the study of tree rings are developed from: Battan, *Weather in Your Life,* 73; Fradin, 33; Schneider and Londer, 127–129; Tufty, 248; Weiner, 246, 249–50.

3. The material and footnotes on the possible connection between

sunspot activity and cyclical drought is developed from: Battan, *Weather*, 75–76; Hardy et al., 162, 165; T. Loftin, 139; Schneider and Londer, 126–127.

4. The material and footnotes on the jet stream are developed from: Lehr et al., 42–43; Weiner, 79.

5. The definitions of La Niña and El Niño, and the material on the former's appearance in 1988 and the latter's in 1983 are developed from: E. Linden, "Big Chill for the Greenhouse," *Time*, October 31, 1988, 90; Mantell and Mantell, 112–14; W. K. Stevens, "Scientists Link '88 Drought to Natural Cycle in Tropical Pacific," *New York Times*, January 3, 1989; K. E. Trenberth, G. W. Branstator, P. A. Arkin, "Origins of the 1988 North American Drought," *Science*, December 23, 1988, 1640–45; Weiner, 79–81.

Chapter Five
Unending Attacks

1. The text material and footnotes on the examples of drought's worldwide appearance throughout history are developed from: Tufty, 239–240.

2. The material on drought and India's Harappan civilization and on other droughts that have struck India is developed from: Dolan, *A Lion in the Sun: The Rise and Fall of the British Empire* (New York: Parents' Magazine Press, 1973), 55; Fradin, 41–42; Tufty, 257–58; Weiner, 99.

3. The text material and footnotes on the Sahara Desert and the world's other major deserts are developed from: Strahler, 333; Tufty, 258–60.

4. The text material and footnotes on drought in North America are developed from: Sanders, 181, 186; Schneider and Londer, 126–27, 385; Tufty, 240, 242–43.

Chapter Six
The Dirty Thirties

1. The text material and footnotes on the drought of the 1930s are developed from: Battan, *Harvesting the Clouds*, 9; D. I. Blumenstock, *The Ocean of Air* (New Brunswick, N.J.: Rutgers University Press, 1959), 81–82; Fradin, 5–14; Loftin, 132–133;

W. L. Neff and M. G. Planer, *World History for a Better World* (Milwaukee: Bruce, 1958), 636, 686–87.

2. The material on the dust storms that struck during the drought is developed from: Battan, *Harvesting*, 9; Johnson, 78; Tufty, 241–42.

3. The material on the blame that humans must take for the dust storms is developed from: M. Burke, *United States History: The Growth of Our Land* (Chicago: American Technical Society, 1957), 353; Hardy et al., 136–37; W. P. Webb, *The Great Plains* (Boston: Ginn, 1931), 343, 375–76.

Chapter Seven
Fighting Back

1. The text material and footnotes on the agricultural practices developed in the 1930s to protect the Great Plains against future drought are developed from: Fradin, 15, 54–55; Schneider and Londer, 385; A. and M. Sutton, *Nature on the Rampage* (Philadelphia: J. B. Lippincott, 1962), 114–16; Tufty, 270–271; Webb, 379.

2. Tufty, 271.

3. H. Thomas, *A History of the World* (New York: Harper & Row, 1979), 92.

4. The material on the development of drought safeguards in antiquity and their continuing use today is developed from: T. A. Bailey, *The American Pageant* (Boston: D. C. Heath, 1956), 824; Fradin, 15, 50–52; Johnson, 79–80; *The 1989 Information Please Almanac* (Boston: Houghton Mifflin, 1989) 585–86.

5. The material on the ideas and ceremonies used to induce drought from the earliest times to the nineteenth century on the Great Plains is developed from: Blumenstock, 246–47; A. and M. Sutton, 121–22; Webb, 377.

Chapter Eight
Fighting Back with Weather Modification

1. The material on the definition of weather modification and the description of its work is developed from: Battan, *Weather in Your Life*, 92–98.

2. The material on the experiments to induce rain with artillery fire and other explosives is developed from: Blumenstock, 247–49; A. and M. Sutton, 95, 119; Webb, 380–81.

3. The material and footnotes on modern weather modification and the development of cloud seeding are developed from: Battan, *Weather*, 92–94, 95, 96–97, 119–20; Hardy et al., 57, 65, 80; Lehr et al., 31; Webb, 382.

Chapter Nine
The Future Enemy

1. The text and footnotes on the global cooling trend and the ice ages of the past are developed from: L. J. Battan, *Weather in Your Life*, 73–74, 198; Blumenstock, 232; Fradin, 57, 60; Hardy et al., 148–149, 152, 156, 157–60; Strahler, 428, 433, 536–41.

2. The text material and footnotes on the greenhouse effect are developed from: Brown, 8–9; Hardy et al., 15, 139, 173, 179; Lehr et al., 6, 8; M. D. Lemonick, "The Heat Is On," *Time*, October 19, 1987, 63; C. Petit, "Why the Earth's Climate Is Changing Dramatically," *San Francisco Chronicle*, August 8, 1988; Petit, "Cutting Trees Contributes to the Greenhouse Effect," *San Francisco Chronicle*, August 8, 1988.

Chapter Ten
Conquering the Future Enemy

1. The material on the national and international programs to reduce the air pollution caused by toxic emissions and other factors is developed from: Brown, 18–19, 108–09; "Developing New Strategies to Minimize the Damage," *San Francisco Chronicle*, August 9, 1988.

2. The material on the preservation and expansion of the world's fresh water supply is developed from: Johnson, 81–84; Loftin, 161; J. F. Lounsbury and L. Ogden, *Earth Science* (New York: Harper & Row, 1969), 256–66; Schneider and Londer, 428; Strahler, 448; Tufty, 269, 279.

3. The material on water conservation measures is developed from: T. Minton, "How Marin Will Limit Water Use," *San Francisco Chronicle*, July 29, 1988; Tufty, 237; *The 1989 Information Please Almanac* (Boston, Houghton, Mifflin, 1989), 154, 168, 281.

BIBLIOGRAPHY

———○———

Bailey, Thomas A. and Kennedy, David M. *The American Pageant*. Lexington, Massachusetts: D.C. Heath and Company, 1983.

Battan, Louis J. *Harvesting the Clouds: Advances in Weather Modification*. New York: Doubleday, 1969.

————. *Weather in Your Life*. New York: W. H. Freeman, 1983.

Blumenstock, David I. *The Ocean of Air*. New Brunswick, N.J.: Rutgers University Press, 1959.

Brown, Lester R., Project Director. *State of the World, 1989: A Worldwatch Institute Report on Progress Toward a Sustainable Society*. New York: W. W. Norton, 1989.

————. "Drought Highlights Decline in Global Food Supplies." *San Francisco Chronicle*, August 17, 1988.

Burke, Merle. *United States History: The Growth of Our Land*. Chicago: American Technical Society, 1957.

Dolan, Edward F. *A Lion in the Sun: The Rise and Fall of the British Empire*. New York: Parent's Magazine Press, 1973.

————. *The Old Farmer's Almanac Book of Weather Lore*. Dublin, N.H.: Yankee Books, 1988.

Fradin, Dennis B. *Disaster! Droughts*. Chicago: Children's Press, 1983.

Hardy, Ralph; Wright, Peter; Kington and Gribbin, John. *The Weather Book*. Boston: Little, Brown, 1982.

Johnson, Thomas P. *When Nature Runs Wild*. Mankato, Minn.: Creative Education Press, 1968.

Johnson, Vance. *Heaven's Tableland: The Dust Bowl Story*. New York: Farrar, Straus, 1947.

Lehr, Paul E.; Burnett, R. W.; and Zim, Herbert S. *Weather*. Racine, Wis.: Western Publishing, 1975.

Lemonick, Michael D. "The Heat Is On," *Time*, October 19, 1987.

Lounsbury, John F., and Ogden, Lawrence. *Earth Science*. New York: Harper & Row, 1969.

Ludlum, David, and the Editors of Blair & Ketchum's Country Journal. *The Country Journal New England Weather Book*. Boston: Houghton Mifflin, 1976.

Micallef, Mary. *Floods and Droughts*. Carthage, Ill.: Good Apple, 1985.

National Geographic Society, Special Publications Division. *Powers of Nature*. Washington, D.C.: National Geographic Society, 1978.

Neff, William Lee, and Planer, Mabel Gertrude. *World History for a Better World*. Milwaukee: Bruce Publishing, 1958.

Rubin, Louis D., Sr., and Duncan, Jim. *The Weather Wizard's Cloud Book*. Chapel Hill, N.C.: Algonquin Books of Chapel Hill, 1970.

Sanders, Ti. *Weather: A User's Guide to the Atmosphere*. South Bend, Ind.: Icarus Press, 1985.

Schneider, Stephen H., and Londer, Randi. *The Coevolution of Climate and Life*. San Francisco: Sierra Club Books, 1984.

Stevens, William K. "Scientists Link '88 Drought to Natural Cycle in Tropical Pacific." *The New York Times*, January 3, 1989.

Strahler, Arthur N. *The Earth Sciences*. New York: Harper & Row, 1963.

Sutton, Ann, and Sutton, Myron. *Nature on the Rampage: A Natural History of the Elements*. Philadelphia: J. B. Lippincott, 1962.

Thomas, Hugh. *A History of the World*. New York: Harper & Row, 1979.

Trenberth, Kevin E.; Branstator, Grant W.; and Arkin, Philip A. "Origins of the 1988 North American Drought." *Science,* December 23, 1988.

Tufty, Barbara. *1001 Questions Answered About Natural Land Disasters.* New York: Dodd, Mead, 1969.

Webb, Walter Prescott. *The Great Plains.* New York: Grosset & Dunlap, 1931.

Weiner, Jonathan. *Planet Earth.* New York: Bantam Books, 1986.

INDEX

—◦—